THE STATES AND THE NATION SERIES, of which this volume is a part, is designed to assist the American people in a serious look at the ideals they have espoused and the experiences they have undergone in the history of the nation. The content of every volume represents the scholarship, experience, and opinions of its author. The costs of writing and editing were met mainly by grants from the National Endowment for the Humanities, a federal agency. The project was administered by the American Association for State and Local History, a nonprofit learned society, working with an Editorial Board of distinguished editors, authors, and historians, whose names are listed below.

Michigan

A Bicentennial History

Bruce Catton

W. W. Norton & Company, Inc.
New York

American Association for State and Local History
Nashville

Portions of this book have appeared earlier, in somewhat different form, in the author's book *Waiting for the Morning Train* (Garden City, N.Y.: Doubleday & Co., Inc., 1972).

Author and publishers make grateful acknowledgment to the Historical Society of Michigan for permission to quote eight lines from a ballad published in George R. Fuller, editor, *Historic Michigan,* 3 vols. (Lansing, Mich.: National Historical Association, Inc., 1924), II:566–567.

Library of Congress Cataloguing-in-Publication Data

Catton, Bruce, 1899–
    Michigan, a Bicentennial history.

    (The States and the Nation series)
    Bibliography: p.
    Includes index.
    1. Michigan—History. I. Title. II. Series:
States and the Nation.
F566.C3   977.4   75–38691
ISBN 0   393   05572   8
            Printed in the United States of America

2 3 4 5 6 7 8 9

To Donald and Alberta Gibb

Contents

Illustrations

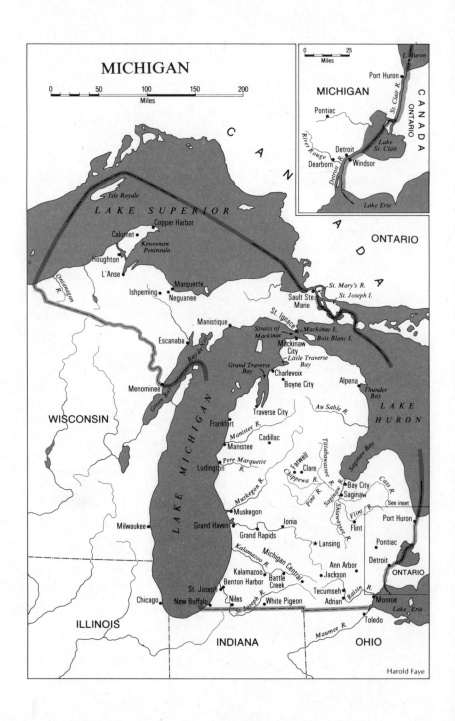

MICHIGAN

0 50 100 150 200
Miles

0 25
Miles

MICHIGAN

Pontiac

L. Huron

Port Huron

Detroit

Dearborn

Windsor

River Rouge

St. Clair R.

Detroit R.

Lake St. Clair

Lake Erie

CANADA

ONTARIO

Isle Royale

LAKE SUPERIOR

Copper Harbor

Calumet

Keweenaw Peninsula

Houghton

L'Anse

Ontonagon R.

Marquette

Ishpeming

Neguanee

St. Mary's R.

St. Joseph I.

Sault Ste. Marie

ONTARIO

CANADA

Manistique

St. Ignace

Mackinac I.

Escanaba

Straits of Mackinac

Bois Blanc I.

Mackinaw City

Little Traverse Bay

Grand Traverse Bay

Charlevoix

Boyne City

Alpena

Thunder Bay

Menominee

Bay de Noc

Green Bay

LAKE MICHIGAN

Traverse City

Au Sable R.

LAKE HURON

WISCONSIN

Frankfort

Manistee R.

Cadillac

Manistee

Pere Marquette R.

Farwell

Clare

Tittabawassee R.

Saginaw Bay

Ludington

Chippewa R.

Pine R.

Saginaw R.

Shiawassee R.

Bay City

Saginaw

Cass R.

See inset

Muskegon R.

Muskegon

Ionia

Flint R.

Flint

Port Huron

Milwaukee

Grand Haven

Grand Rapids

★ Lansing

Pontiac

Detroit

Kalamazoo R.

Michigan Central

ONTARIO

Kalamazoo

Battle Creek

Ann Arbor

Jackson

Chicago

St. Joseph

Benton Harbor

Niles

White Pigeon

St. Joseph R.

Tecumseh

Adrian

Raisin R.

Monroe

Lake Erie

New Buffalo

ILLINOIS

INDIANA

Maumee R.

OHIO

Toledo

Harold Faye

ACKNOWLEDGMENTS

I am deeply indebted to a number of people for advice, suggestions, factual information, or simply for words of encouragement. Specifically, I must extend my thanks to these people:

Howard Peckham, Director of the William L. Clements Library of the University of Michigan, for helpful pointers in connection with the financing of the early automobile industry.

Lawrence Gustin, of the *Flint Journal,* for sending me his excellent biography of William C. Durant, founder of General Motors.

Carlton F. Wells, professor emeritus of English at the University of Michigan, who steered me onto two delightful books on Michigan, which, unaccountably, I had missed: John Bartlow Martin's *Call It North Country* and Della Lutes's *A Country Kitchen.*

Charles E. Cleland, Curator of Anthropology, The Museum, Michigan State University, for helpful information on the pre-Columbian distribution and movements of Michigan's Indians.

Mrs. Madeleine Lindsay, of Detroit, for sending me copies of her fine vignettes of pioneer history and for giving me a graphic explanation of what the early settlers meant when they said that a family had been "grubbing out a living" in the cut-over country.

Ralph W. Muncy of Ann Arbor, for a stimulating letter discussing our society's dependence on a "one-direction" transportation system and the possible effects of our ultimate loss of mobility.

Judge William R. Peterson, of Cadillac, who discussed with me some of the ins and outs of pioneer days in Wexford County as described in his fine book, *The View from Courthouse Hill.*

Catherine Stebbins, of Frankfort, for sharing with me the fruits of her extensive knowledge of the early development of the Michilimackinac country and the founding of St. Ignace.

Tom Riordan, of the *Jackson Citizen Patriot,* for sending me Clara Waldron's interesting book, *One Hundred Years a Country Town.*

July 1975   *Bruce Catton*

Invitation to the Reader

IN 1807, former President John Adams argued that a complete history of the American Revolution could not be written until the history of change in each state was known, because the principles of the Revolution were as various as the states that went through it. Two hundred years after the Declaration of Independence, the American nation has spread over a continent and beyond. The states have grown in number from thirteen to fifty. And democratic principles have been interpreted differently in every one of them.

We therefore invite you to consider that the history of your state may have more to do with the bicentennial review of the American Revolution than does the story of Bunker Hill or Valley Forge. The Revolution has continued as Americans extended liberty and democracy over a vast territory. John Adams was right: the states are part of that story, and the story is incomplete without an account of their diversity.

The Declaration of Independence stressed life, liberty, and the pursuit of happiness; accordingly, it shattered the notion of holding new territories in the subordinate status of colonies. The Northwest Ordinance of 1787 set forth a procedure for new states to enter the Union on an equal footing with the old. The Federal Constitution shortly confirmed this novel means of building a nation out of equal states. The step-by-step process through which territories have achieved self-government and national representation is among the most important of the Founding Fathers' legacies.

The method of state-making reconciled the ancient conflict between liberty and empire, resulting in what Thomas Jefferson called an empire for liberty. The system has worked and remains unaltered, despite enormous changes that have taken place in the nation. The country's extent and variety now surpass anything the patriots of '76 could likely have imagined. The United States has changed from an agrarian republic into a highly industrial and urban democracy, from a fledgling nation into a major world power. As Oliver Wendell Holmes remarked in 1920, the creators of the nation could not have seen completely how it and its constitution and its states would develop. Any meaningful review in the bicentennial era must consider what the country has become, as well as what it was.

The new nation of equal states took as its motto *E Pluribus Unum*—"out of many, one." But just as many peoples have become Americans without complete loss of ethnic and cultural identities, so have the states retained differences of character. Some have been superficial, expressed in stereotyped images— big, boastful Texas, "sophisticated" New York, "hillbilly" Arkansas. Other differences have been more real, sometimes instructively, sometimes amusingly; democracy has embraced Huey Long's Louisiana, bilingual New Mexico, unicameral Nebraska, and a Texas that once taxed fortunetellers and spawned politicians called "Woodpecker Republicans" and "Skunk Democrats." Some differences have been profound, as when South Carolina secessionists led other states out of the Union in opposition to abolitionists in Massachusetts and Ohio. The result was a bitter Civil War.

The Revolution's first shots may have sounded in Lexington and Concord; but fights over what democracy should mean and who should have independence have erupted from Pennsylvania's Gettysburg to the "Bleeding Kansas" of John Brown, from the Alamo in Texas to the Indian battles at Montana's Little Bighorn. Utah Mormons have known the strain of isolation; Hawaiians at Pearl Harbor, the terror of attack; Georgians during Sherman's march, the sadness of defeat and devastation. Each state's experience differs instructively; each adds understanding to the whole.

The purpose of this series of books is to make that kind of understanding accessible, in a way that will last in value far beyond the bicentennial fireworks. The series offers a volume on every state, plus the District of Columbia—fifty-one, in all.

Each book contains, besides the text, a view of the state through eyes other than the author's—a "photographer's essay," in which a skilled photographer presents his own personal perceptions of the state's contemporary flavor.

We have asked authors not for comprehensive chronicles, nor for research monographs or new data for scholars. Bibliographies and footnotes are minimal. We have asked each author for a summing up—interpretive, sensitive, thoughtful, individual, even personal—of what seems significant about his or her state's history. What distinguishes it? What has mattered about it, to its own people and to the rest of the nation? What has it come to now?

To interpret the states in all their variety, we have sought a variety of backgrounds in authors themselves and have encouraged variety in the approaches they take. They have in common only these things: historical knowledge, writing skill, and strong personal feelings about a particular state. Each has wide latitude for the use of the short space. And if each succeeds, it will be by offering you, in your capacity as a *citizen* of a state *and* of a nation, stimulating insights to test against your own.

James Morton Smith
General Editor

Michigan

The Everlasting Road

$\mathscr{M}$ICHIGAN has never really had a present moment. It has a mysterious past and an incalculable future, attractive and terrifying by turns, but the moment where the two meet is always a time of transition. The state is caught between yesterday and tomorrow, existing less for itself than for what it leads to; it is a road whose ends are distorted by imagination and imperfect knowledge. The great American feeling of being en route—to the unknown, to something new, to the fantastic reality that must lie beyond the mists—is perfectly represented here. If the nation is now wholly given over to the making and using of highways, here, maybe, is where the process began.

Probably it is characteristic that the first white men who saw Michigan looked past it, in the belief that they were entering China, with Marco Polo and Kublai Khan haunting the land just beyond Lake Michigan. Jean Nicolet, the Frenchman who cruised the straits from Lake Huron and who donned a mandarin's robes when he went ashore at Green Bay, in the belief that the fresh-water seas had led him to the Orient, was the first in a long procession. He did not find what he expected to find, but he at least learned that the world was a great deal bigger than he had thought it was. The new country had taught him what it has taught other men since then: the horizon is always receding; but although you can never reach it, you have to keep trying. It does not take astronomers to recognize the expanding universe.

It began to be visible when men venturing into the empty land recognized and responded to the reality of unlimited opportunity.

So Nicolet looked for Asia west by south of Mackinac, a week away by birchbark canoe, and he failed to find it because he was half a world off the mark, a good man groping in the mysterious lake's golden twilight for something that was not there. Étienne Brulé, who went out ahead of him, had better luck. He hunted a fantastic intangible, found it, made the most of it, and vanished at last into bloodstained legend, his final thoughts unrecorded. He wanted to get to the fabulous back-of-beyond—to discard everything he had been taught in seventeenth-century France and find out how it would go with a man who followed total loneliness into the loneliest forest on earth—and he did precisely what he set out to do, which is more than most men ever do. The result was something he had not foreseen. Discarding civilization and making himself totally uncivilized, he nevertheless dragged civilization after him, which is why no one today can go where he went and see what he saw. By escaping into the wholly primitive, he helped to destroy it.

So Brulé is worth a second look. Born in France, he came to America in 1608, a bright lad of sixteen on the staff of Samuel Champlain, who was lieutenant-governor of New France and founder of Quebec: a man powerfully moved by the acquisitive instinct. Champlain was drawn to the American interior by the certain knowledge that it contained much wealth in the form of furs, by persistent rumors that big lumps of pure copper lay about in the trackless forest waiting to be picked up, and by the unfounded belief that a short road to the Far East was there to be opened. In 1610, he went up the St. Lawrence to the mouth of the Richelieu River to talk to some Algonquin tribesmen from the lake country and see what he could learn. He took Brulé, who was learning to interpret the Indian tongues for him.

Champlain learned just enough to sharpen his enthusiasm. The Indians assured him that there was a vast lake up there—it might indeed be the frozen sea of the Far North, or an arm of the Pacific, or some other body of water on which Frenchmen might sail to riches and glory. They confirmed what he already knew about the incredible plenty of furbearing animals, told him that the stories about copper were quite true, and invited him to go up-country with them and see, himself.

Champlain had other engagements, so he could not go up to the legendary wilderness; but he did crack its shell, and he used Brulé as the sharp tool-steel probe to reach in and pry the kernel loose. He told the Indians that he would like to send this young man with them, to spend a year living as they lived, learning their language and their ways and coming to know the far-off lakes and rivers and forests. The Indians were reluctant. They knew very well the many ways in which death can strike in a northern winter, and they feared that, if something happened to Brulé, Champlain would think it was their fault and punish them; they were very much in awe of this white man and his firearms. Champlain talked them out of their fears, and at last they made a deal; they would take Brulé to the high country, and Champlain would take one of their young men back to France. After a year, they would all meet at the mouth of the Richelieu, and the young men would rejoin their own people.

The interesting thing about this is that Brulé himself begged Champlain to send him to the wilderness. It had bugged him, and it drew him on to a mutual catastrophe. Even the Quebec of that day was closer to the primeval forest than anyone today can ever be, but Brulé saw something far beyond, and it was this far-beyond that he wanted. So away he went—up the Ottawa River, over Lake Nipissing, down the French River to Georgian Bay, along the coast to the pocket where the land runs north-northwest again to Lake Huron, which is deep and wide and blue and cold and deadly—and he was the first white man to see any of this, the first to escape entirely from the tight limits of Europe, the first one free to explore himself under the guise of exploring a new land. This is very strong wine. It is much as if, today, a man landed on the moon and found the gates of fantasy wide open, with an enchanted garden waiting to be entered; if he went in, he might die there, and he knew this perfectly well; but as a young man, he also knew the final value of life better than the old do, so in he went, and there he died, and if he could have come back afterward, he would not have undone any of it.

So Brulé spent a year with the Hurons and adapted zestfully. They were dirty and verminous, and they lived in drafty houses full of smoke and noise, their food was atrocious, and they were haunted by hideous dreams, and very rarely in their lives were they really comfortable. But much the same could be said of most Europeans at that time, and Brulé apparently enjoyed every minute of it. At the end of the year, there was the reunion, and the two hostages were returned to their own people. It is reported that the Indian who had lived in France went back to the high country somewhat against his will, telling his white friends that his life in France had spoiled him for the wilderness. It is certain that Brulé felt the same way in reverse; the wilderness had taken him over, and he was no longer a European, so that the rest of his life goes off into the hollow places under the tall pine trees as he tried to make an adjustment that was rewarding but impossible.

Brulé had many adventures, obscure and apparently pointless. He wandered all over the high country, getting into Lake Superior and coasting along its magnificent and deadly shores, seeing the copper country without seeing the copper and going to the great harbor that lies under the long sand bar behind which Duluth now climbs the hills to breath-taking beauty, never knowing that the world's greatest deposit of iron ore lay just a few miles up-country. To do him justice, he would not have cared at all if he had known it. He went back to the Huron country and turned south and east; got into up-state New York and was caught by a party of Iroquois, who prepared to torture him to death and began pulling out his beard by the handful, just to give him a foretaste. Brulé threatened them with the wrath of the Great Spirit; at which moment, in the most unbelievable story-book fashion, a thunderhead that had climbed the sunny sky unnoticed exploded in a great blast of bumping noise and blinding fire, so that the Iroquois were suddenly converted and tried to atone. They untied him, gave him a big dinner, and sent him on his way with their best wishes.

He kept on going; went over into what is now northeastern Pennsylvania and followed the Susquehanna down to the Chesapeake, got back north alive, checked in now and then with Champlain, and returned to the high country, where he lived here and there. It is easier to say this than it could possibly have been to do it. He was not just living among the Indians: he was living among an all but infinite number of different tribes of Indians, some of whom felt *this* way, while others felt *that* way. Make friends with one tribe, and you make enemies of another, and your life is poised on a knife edge, all the time. Also, the Indians had taboos, superstitions, and social codes that nobody knew about, and a man could lose his life if he pushed too hard against any of them. The same thing, of course, was pretty much true in Europe in those days, but a European at least knew how to keep score there; in the high country about the big lakes, he had to find out the scoring system as he went along, and if he did it wrong the penalty he had to pay was final.

For years, Brulé played the game very well; that is, he stayed alive and had exactly the kind of life he wanted to have, becoming—as happened afterward to many another man who wandered away from the settlements—more Indian than the Indians. He seems to have disconnected himself completely from all his old ties. The English fought the French, and Brulé did not know which side he was on, going with the English for a time and then at last picking up the old threads again with the French. In the end, he managed to make a fatal mistake in some dealing with the Indians; if he could forget that he was a white man, they could not, and at last—in a Huron town called Toanché, whose site is lost in the gloom of wilderness prehistory—the red men found that they were mortally tired of him. They clubbed him to death, and then, according to legend, they ate him; and so, in 1632, his story ended forever.

The story is obscure all the way, and Brulé may have been more the result of a historic process than one of its chief causes; an obbligato, so to speak, heard now and then while the principal theme is carried by a more robust instrument. Yet his direct connection with what finally happened is unmistakable. He was one of the means by which Champlain drew Indians from the high country to Montreal by the hundred, their canoes deeply laden with furs. Also, Brulé had set an example. Men in the French towns along the St. Lawrence learned about the high country at least in part because of Brulé. Much more important, when the rigid monopoly that controlled the fur trade grew irksome and impelled lawless men to go into the wilderness and poach in a continental preserve, what Brulé had done was like a beacon. The long trip from Montreal to the Straits of Mackinac and beyond was hard and dangerous in the extreme, and the life one had to live after that trip had been made was even more so—but Brulé had done it, even though he finally paid with his life for it; and what he had done, other men might also do. He had set a notable pattern, and the *coureurs de bois* followed it.

By the edict of the French king, rigorously enforced by his agents in New France, the fur trade was to be tightly controlled, and no outsider was to be allowed to get into it. The identities of the monopolists changed from time to time, but they all found this rule hard to enforce, because the untracked forest of the lake country was a very bad place to run a monopoly. This became evident quite early in the game, when the monopoly was scouting the country for trails, tribes, and riches. Champlain sent Nicolet west in 1634, to see whether Peking did not perhaps lie just beyond Green Bay; but he was much more interested in furs, because, while the road to China might or might not be there, an incalculable fortune in furs was there beyond a doubt; and if Nicolet was disappointed in his quest, Champlain assuredly was not. Brulé had already shown that a lone man, sufficiently daring, could go to the lakes; Nicolet's futile venture showed that a whole expedition could go, added numbers meaning greater safety. Instead of having an Indian tribe bring all the furs to Montreal—the untaught red man understood the uses of monopoly just as well as the Frenchman did—the French could go to the wilderness, deal with all the tribes, and collect the raw materials at the source.

The monopoly still needed individual traders who could go roving far into the interior to get furs, and there soon developed a license system under which twenty-five license-holders were obliged to send out two canoes apiece, with three men and assorted trade goods in each canoe. This brought in a gratifying quantity of furs; it also meant that the Michigan country began to have visitors, who went cross-country with the spirited pertinacity of born salesmen operating in a seller's own market to persuade men of the stone age that the white man's tools, weapons, pots, and blankets were better than anything he could make for himself. This was self-evident: they *were* better, infinitely better, and the fact that the red man was being royally exploited meant very little because the trade did bring him things that he very much wanted and could not otherwise get. So he paid a beaver skin for two hatchets or two pounds of powder, paid four for one woolen blanket, and spent six to buy a gun, and innocently supposed that he had the best of the bargain.

The traders were not the only visitors. Hard on their heels, or in some cases well ahead of them, came men who were infinitely the traders' superiors in every point you could easily think of—in brains, in morals, in courage, and in the desire to give the Indian more than would be taken from him in return: the Black Robes, Jesuit missionaries, who set a strange new fashion by trying to do something *for* the red man, rather than *to* him. (It was a fashion that somehow never caught on, in Michigan or elsewhere.) Long before the crown's representatives in the east knew how the land lay or how the rivers ran in the high country, the Jesuits were finding out, joining a passion for saving lost souls to a deep and abiding curiosity about the geography of the region where the lost souls were temporarily in residence. Along with everything else, they were matchless explorers, and they left their mark on the land in a way the king's men never did.

Where the Saint Mary's River brings the overflow from Lake Superior down to the lower lakes, it goes foaming and splashing over picturesque rapids—the Sault de Ste. Marie, as the French said it—and because the water here harbored wholly fantastic numbers of whitefish, which are the best fish to eat anyone ever caught, and because the narrow river here offered men a good way to get from the east side of the Great Lakes chain to the west side, the ground just west of the Sault was a congregating

place for Indians since before time began. Traders coming from
Montreal learned to head for the Sault early in the game, and
the Jesuits were not far behind them. As early as 1641, we hear
of two of the Black Robes preaching to a congregation of 2,000
Indians there by the rapids; by 1667, they had established a mission there; and a year later, a dedicated priest named Jacques
Marquette was assigned to this mission. At this time, a town
grew up around the mission: the oldest permanently occupied
settlement in Michigan, Sault Ste. Marie, known universally as
the Soo, a place that Henry Clay, many years later, unsym-
pathetically described as "the remotest settlement in the United
States, if not in the moon." By its mere existence, the Soo indicated that the brief portage that took *voyageurs* up to Lake
Superior was beginning to be important. Mostly, the traders
who went into this lake—a lake so vast, Brulé had reported, that
the Indians on the St. Mary's had never seen the end of it, nor
heard of anyone who had—stuck close to the south shore as
they made their way westward. This was partly because men
who ventured on Lake Superior in bark canoes had to stay close
to the shore, on one side or the other: they had to be able to get
on dry land quickly if the lake began to kick up rough. But
partly, too, they stayed near this coast because the great copper
country was supposed to be in there somewhere. Also, this most
forbidding and desolate of shore lines was not wholly savage
country; the Jesuits had two missions there, that of La Pointe,
on Chequemagon Bay, far to the west, and L'Anse, at the base
of the Keweenaw Peninsula. Father Claude Jean Allouez, who
founded La Pointe Mission, brought back to the Soo some actual samples of native copper, picked up on the Keweenaw; the
copper country was beginning to emerge from the haze, although more than 150 years would pass before anybody did
anything about it.

Anyone who looks back at Michigan's beginnings is bound to
let his gaze linger on Father Marquette. Wholly committed to
his calling, the man was at the same time a born explorer, and
he helped unroll the map for the lookers and seekers who would
come later. If Michigan is indeed the road to the future, he
showed that love for one's fellows can take a man along that

road just as brightly as greed and an eye for the main chance,
which usually seem to be the primary driving forces. He was the
sort of man whom it is pleasant to remember.

Marquette was transferred from the Soo to La Pointe, where
he found trouble. The mission was new, small, and weak, the
warlike Sioux whose country was nearby were threatening to
destroy the mission and everyone in it, and the little congregation was in terror. Marquette doubtless would have welcomed
martyrdom for himself, but he could hardly welcome it for his
charges, who, as recent proselytes, were presumably weak in
the faith; so he took everybody east to the Soo, down the St.
Mary's, and west into the Straits, to make a new mission, St.
Ignace, at Michilimackinac.

Michilimackinac is a stumbling block for anyone who writes
or talks about Michigan. There are innumerable ways to spell it,
there is argument over its meaning, and there is no logic whatever to its pronunciation; on top of which, it does not stay put
properly as a historic place should. Before Marquette's time, the
name was applied to the entire Straits area, which was the
Michilimackinac country. Today, mercifully abbreviated to
Mackinac, the name is applied only to the island out in the
Straits—a beautiful place, the only spot in the state of Michigan
where no automobiles are allowed. South of the island, at the
tip of the lower peninsula, there is a village named Mackinaw
City; perversely, here the name is spelled the way the name of
the island is pronounced. In any case, when Marquette and his
charges arrived, the great name was being applied to a more or
less intermittent and informal trading center that had come into
existence around a little bay on the east side of a point on the
north shore of the Straits. Later, it meant the Mackinaw City
area, where a notable fort was built, and still later it meant the
island, where there was another notable fort. Men said that
Michilimackinac meant "great turtle," in the Ottawas' language, but an Ottawa chief in the nineteenth century said that
this was not so at all; the name came, he insisted, from a small
tribe that originally lived on the island, a folk called the Mi-she-
ne-mackinaw-go; and anyone who wants to go into it more
deeply is quite free to do so.

So Marquette built the mission chapel of St. Ignace on a fine hilltop north of the Straits; and, by intent or by accident, he had picked a strategic point in space and in time. After years in which north-country affairs more or less took care of themselves, the faraway French government had decided to establish a real presence there. Regular troops were sent over all the way from France; and about the time Marquette got back to the Soo from La Pointe, there was an elaborate ceremony beside the flashing rapids of the St. Mary's. A huge cross was erected on the bank, military and clergy formed ranks in full regalia, fleur-de-lis banners lifted to the cold wind from Lake Superior, bemused Indians looked on impressed but not understanding; and a functionary in uniform proclaimed that all of this country—what they could see and what they could not see, extending even to the northern and western oceans—belonged now and henceforward to King Louis XIV. Where Brulé had gone, all lawless and without restraint, the rule of the Sun King had arrived with professional soldiers to enforce it; and so, when Marquette built his new mission, the soldiers came in on his heels and built Fort de Buade nearby for his protection. In next to no time, the fort and mission were known as Michilimackinac, first in a notable progression.

The spot where the fur traders had been holding their get-togethers took its name from Marquette's mission, St. Ignace, and bears the name to this day, with shops and stores and houses lining the street by the bay-side just as the traders' shacks had done generations ago. But if this little settlement was permanent, neither the fort nor the mission endured; in the fullness of time, both of them disappeared altogether, and many years afterward, when a great bridge was built across the Straits, no one could be sure just where fort and mission had been. Apparently, the mission had been built on a flat-topped hill or butte at a place called Castle Rock, three miles north of the present town, with the fort at the mouth of a creek a mile south of the mission; and however all of that may be, Marquette followed the routine of a missionary priest for two years or more. Then, in the fall of 1673, Louis Jolliet showed up bearing letters, and everything was changed.

Marquette clearly wanted a change. He was as devout as ever, as dedicated as a priest or layman could possibly be, but the explorer who went hand in hand with the missionary beneath his black robe was growing restless. At La Pointe, Allouez had collected many reports about a great river in the west, flowing south, possibly to the south seas, and when Marquette replaced him, Marquette had collected more, earnestly seeking human and divine sanction to do what he ardently wanted to do: go and see where this river was and where it went, adding many new details to the map of New France and at the same time bringing salvation to benighted red men who otherwise would not get it and would be lost forever. Now, here was Jolliet, with letters telling Marquette that he could go.

Jolliet was a good man to go with, a rover who had turned from fur trader into explorer. Two years earlier, he had gone by canoe from the Soo all the way to Lake Erie—the first European, apparently, to make the Detroit River passage down from the high country. Now he had been commissioned to find out just where the Mississippi was—if indeed it existed in these parts at all and was not just part of the distorted fable that had put the Grand Khan in Wisconsin—and he bore formal authorization from Marquette's superior for Marquette to go with him. It is clear that this was not just a favor for a deserving priest. Marquette was not being given a free ride; he probably knew more about the way to get from the Great Lakes to the Big River than any man alive, except for some anonymous Indians hidden in the woods southwest of Chequemagon, and he had an essential part to play. He was still a missionary, but now he was a full-fledged explorer, as well, and on this wide swing into the totally unknown, he would save souls for God and also extend the physical dominion of the king of France. He was well qualified for both tasks.

The existence of the Mississippi, of course, was well known; the existence, that is, of *a* Mississippi, de Soto's river, far to the south, which ran down to the Gulf of Mexico and probably belonged to the king of Spain. But it was important for the French to know whether this great river the Indians talked about was indeed de Soto's river in its upper reaches or some totally different stream, one that possibly ran all the way across the Southwest to the South Sea. So little was known about the North American interior that anything might be possible, and with the Sun King in an expansionist mood, it was necessary to be certain. So, on a day in the early spring of 1673, an important expedition set out—Jolliet and Marquette in two birchbark canoes, with half a dozen assorted *voyageur* types for helpers and a modest amount of parched corn and dried meat for rations, paddling down from Michilimackinac to assert the rule of Louis XIV in a deep land no European had ever seen.

They went down west of Lake Michigan, going south and west from Green Bay by the Fox River, over to the Wisconsin by easy portages, and on at last to the Mississippi, which they reached in mid-June. They struck it where it is wide, bordered by high bluffs, as impressive to see as one of the world's great rivers ought to be, and here were two of the world's great explorers, come to have a look. They found Indian villages as they went downstream, and the Indians were uniformly friendly; the Indians did not yet know what the opening of this river was going to do to them, and anyhow Marquette was a man people were friendly to by instinct. It is recorded that, when they stopped in what is now Iowa, the white men were fed a huge quantity of corn, which is quite as it should be, the corn belt announcing itself far ahead of time. On and on they went, and at last—they had reached the mouth of the Arkansas River—it was obvious that the great river was not going to slice off toward the southwest; like it or not, they were on de Soto's Mississippi, and if they kept on going, they would probably run into Spaniards and get thrown into prison, so they turned around and headed north. They had made one of the world's momentous discoveries, and the Michigan wilderness was no longer isolated in mystery and great darkness; it could be bound and defined now, its limits charted and described, its ultimate destruction certain.

They went north through the Illinois country—where the Indians were greatly taken with Marquette and begged him to stay with them, and he had to say that he could not, but that he would return—and they got to Lake Michigan, near where Chicago is now, and went coasting up the west shore, portaging over at last to Green Bay. Here they separated, Jolliet going on to lower Canada to make his report to Governor Frontenac, while Marquette rested for a while before he went on to St. Ignace. The Lord who had given this priest the spirit of the explorer had somehow failed to give him the physique that ought to go with it. Marquette had finished a three-thousand-mile journey that was physical hardship all the way, and he was just too frail to take it.

He got back to St. Ignace at last and wrote a detailed account of the trip. It was as well that he did so, because, on the way to Quebec, Jolliet took a spill when his canoe was upset in the St. Lawrence rapids; Jolliet survived, but all his papers and charts were lost, and what the world finally knew about the discovery of the upper Mississippi came to depend almost entirely on Marquette's journal.

The explorer had had his day, and now the missionary took over again. Marquette had promised the Illinois Indians that he would return, and return he did, in 1674. He toiled manfully in this vineyard, but what he had demanded of his body had been just too much for him; he fell ill, and he knew that this was going to be the end—he was two or three thousand miles and probably a couple of centuries, as well, away from the medical care he needed—and at last he set out for St. Ignace again, a stricken priest with two Indian helpers in a canoe, heading up the eastern side of Lake Michigan. He promised the Illinois people that he would send a man down to take his place, but nobody could really replace him; and besides, he never got back to the mission. Along the way, he saw that the end was at hand and had his helpers take him ashore at the mouth of a little river. They built a miserable hut of birchbark for him, he composed himself, made his peace with God—the *pourparlers* could not have been very extensive—and went to cross the final river of all. The Indians buried him by the lake; a year or so later, they returned, dug up his bones, and got what was left of him back to St. Ignace for Christian burial.

Whether he meant to do so or not, Marquette had opened a great door to let light into the wilderness, the wilderness whose protection was the darkness that made it invisible to desirous men. Now one utterly unlike Marquette came on to swing the door open even wider: Robert Cavelier, Sieur de La Salle, who had been trained to be a Jesuit but who discovered in time that he really wanted to go adventuring, not for souls, but for riches and worldly power and so did not belong in an order whose members took the vow of poverty. La Salle came over from France in 1666, at the age of twenty-three, made a trip to the high country, saw infinite possibilities, and laid immense plans. He got the support of Governor Frontenac, who believed that the Jesuits were becoming too powerful and wanted to see a layman overshadow them, and he endorsed La Salle's idea—to set up a chain of forts on the lakes, along the Ohio, and on the Mississippi, to follow the big river all the way to the Gulf and plant a colony there, to develop the fur trade and suppress the outlaw traders, while saving the whole vast interior of the continent for the king of France and for his agent La Salle; all this, of course, to the confusion of the English and the Spanish, who would move into this land of riches if they got half a chance. Clearly, La Salle was half fortune-hunter and half empire-builder, a Cecil Rhodes born in the wrong century on the wrong continent; he had no luck at all, but he did have a perverse talent for making enemies, and in the end he lost his life, and his dream died with him. But while he lasted, he made things happen.

Sending a group of traders out to Lake Michigan a year in advance to collect furs for him, La Salle got to the lower end of Lake Erie in 1679 and built a 45-ton ship, which he named the *Griffon*. A small craft, as commercial cargo carriers go, it was the first vessel other than a canoe ever to touch the water above Niagara Falls. In the *Griffon,* he cruised up Lake Erie, up the Detroit River and Lake St. Clair and the St. Clair River, all the way up Lake Huron and past Michilimackinac to Washington Island, at the entrance to Green Bay. (If it means anything, the rock-strewn passage between island and mainland is known to this day as the Door of Death Passage.) The advance men had furs waiting, and *Griffon* got her pay load. She was to take this back to the lower end of Lake Erie, and the furs would be por-

taged to the Ontario level and taken on by canoe to Montreal. The money thus earned would finance La Salle's next step, and *Griffon* would sail west and rejoin him at the southern end of Lake Michigan.

The furs earned no money for anyone, because *Griffon* went missing, with all hands—first of many shipwrecks on the Great Lakes. Equinoctial storms on Lake Michigan can be violent, and one blew up just after *Griffon* sailed, and that is all anyone knows about it, except that neither ship nor men were ever seen again. The story haunts the imagination: one frail ship, overborne by tempest on an uncharted sea where there were no other ships, no light-houses, no harbors of refuge, no rescuing Coast Guards—no possible chance of help for a ship that could not make it, nothing left but the ultimate darkness at the end of the passage on a shoreless sea.

After this, La Salle was on the road to disaster, although it took him several years to get there. Faithfully following the trail of Jolliet and Marquette, he reached the Gulf of Mexico, named and claimed for King Louis the great land of Louisiana, was named viceroy of this vast dominion—and, for all his striving, was killed by mutineers and got nothing more than a nameless grave in a salt-water swamp somewhere along the Gulf Coast. Before it came to this, he had a few lines to add to the Michigan story.

He waited for *Griffon* at the mouth of the St. Joseph River, far down the Michigan coast of Lake Michigan near the bend in the land that one day would lead to Gary, Indiana Harbor, and Chicago, staining the sky with smoke; and here he learned that *Griffon* had vanished. With his great lieutenant, Henri de Tonty—a veteran of the European wars who had lost a hand fighting in Flanders and had replaced it with a sharp iron hook, which impressed the Indians most fantastically—La Salle went up the St. Joseph, portaged over the low height of land to the Kankakee, and went on down to the Illinois and finally to the Mississippi, where he had many adventures. Before leaving, he built a log stockade fort at the mouth of the St. Joseph, naming it Fort Miami. (The St. Joseph then was known, briefly, as the Miami, because it flowed through the land of the Miami Indians, whose name ultimately was seized by real estate men and transferred to Florida, where it became a hothouse plant all spangled with winter-resort hotels.)

A little later, La Salle concluded that it was time to go back to Montreal and check in with the authorities, so he returned to the mouth of the St. Joseph to go east. Here he found that the hired hands he had left in charge of Fort Miami had grown restless and, thus restless, had burned the fort and gone off to parts unknown; so he set off eastward and, by canoe and on foot, crossed the whole of the lower peninsula of Michigan, coming out at last where Detroit is now and going on from there to Montreal.

From all of which a gleam of light strikes us: La Salle had used a somewhat roundabout but nevertheless convenient route to get from Lake Michigan to the Illinois country and, on his return, he had known just how to go 200 miles east by north to strike the Detroit River; which obviously means that this untracked wilderness had, in fact, been tracked, by men who drew no maps and wrote no memoirs but who nevertheless had been around. The lawless *coureurs de bois,* spiritual heirs of lawless old Brulé, had maps in their heads. They had gone up the rivers and through the forests, past the brief prairie openings of southern Michigan, and on to every place that looked as if it might be interesting. The tremendous forest that weighted down this land was their back yard, they were at home in it, and if a man wanted to go from the mouth of the St. Joseph to New Orleans or Detroit (neither place, to be sure, existing as yet), they could tell him how to do it. Like Brulé, they loved the wilderness and would live nowhere else; and, like him, they had doomed it, and without knowing it had devised its destruction.

It was an involved progression that led Michigan from cold postglacial fog to the superheated twentieth century. Many of the steps seem unrelated. The significance of some of fate's moves is not immediately apparent. One item that helped shape Michigan's destiny was the dire trouble that befell the fur monopoly. As monopolies sometimes do, it grew clumsy as it grew great and finally lost control, not only of the outsiders whom it tried to obliterate, but even of its own members. By the closing

years of the seventeenth century, it was displaying the worst fault a monopoly can have: it was losing money.

The trouble was the *coureur de bois,* the free trader, the same who had amassed the knowledge needed by such empire builders as La Salle; or perhaps the real trouble was the belief that, in an enormous forest offering easy wealth and no law whatever, it would be possible for anybody to exercise the slightest authority over the spiritual descendants of Étienne Brulé.

These men, by now numerous as pine trees along the Muskegon, had gone totally out of hand, because the high country was a long way from Montreal and an even longer way from Versailles. They shamelessly and without restraint gave the Indians brandy. This was morally wrong, because it debauched the noble red man and deprived him of his nobility; it was legally unacceptable because it meant that the woods runners got quantities of furs at bargain prices. No one could stop it. Champlain had tried, Bishop Laval had forbidden the liquor trade under penalty of excommunication, and in 1679 great Louis himself had outlawed it in the sternest terms, but none of this made any difference. The law denying brandy to the Indians had become a dead letter.

So had the law that only licensed men could trade in the high country. The woods runners of course were outlaws to begin with, and in the very nature of things acted as if this law did not exist, but they were not the only unlicensed traders. Apparently, every Frenchman who came to the lakes was trading,'even the soldiers themselves, who had been sent there to enforce the law. At some posts, it was said, most soldiers did practically no military duty, devoting themselves to trade and cutting their officers in on the profits. In desperation, the authorities offered amnesty to all illicit traders who would return to honest ways and sent men to the north country to bring the traders into line—only to find that the emissaries themselves promptly took to trade and became as bad as the men they were supposed to reform.

The result of all of this, naturally, was that a perfect flood of furs went downstream to Montreal. The price of beaver dropped so far that the monopoly had warehouses full of skins that simply lay in storage and rotted because it did not pay to send them to France. This was beyond bearing, and in 1696 King Louis ordered all traders and soldiers withdrawn from the high country. The missionaries might stay if they liked, but everybody else must come back to lower Canada.

The king took this step at the urgent request of the monopolists, who were behaving as blindly and disastrously as the railroad magnates of the 1960s who sought to remedy declining traffic by cutting service to the bone. One man who saw things differently was the commandant at Fort de Buade, at Michilimackinac: Sieur Antoine de La Mothe Cadillac, who saw the Michigan problem from a fresh viewpoint.

Cadillac had become commandant in 1694, exceptional among the men who came west in that he never looked at this country solely as a place to get furs, and found the Indians interesting in their own right and not just as hired hands for the traders. He considered the Indians descendants of the Ten Lost Tribes of Israel, as a matter of fact; he liked Indian food and wrote an informed and interesting study of Indian ways as he had observed them from the fort. When the edict for abandonment of the high country came out, Cadillac recognized it as disastrous folly, and after dutifully withdrawing the garrison, he hastened to the governor to protest; went, in the end, all the way to France, where he took his protest to King Louis.

His protest became effective because he had a new idea to present: stop treating this country as a mere outpost, he said in effect, and plant a genuine colony here; bring in farmers and artisans, develop towns, and urge the Indians to cluster about them. The Indians will bring in furs, and they will also, simply through constant exposure, absorb the white man's religion and adjust themselves to his ways. Treated thus, this country can support itself. Instead of being a constant drain on the King's strength, it will be self-reliant and eventually a source of strength for him to call on. Also, neither the English nor the Iroquois (both of whom definitely had designs on the Michigan area) will be able to make headway against it.

Cadillac was persuasive, and what he said made sense even in Versailles, and he made his point. And so, in the summer of

1701, leading fifty soldiers, fifty traders and artisans, and two priests, he left Montreal, went up the Ottawa, over to Lake Huron, down through the St. Clair River and lake, and on into the lower river, where he built Fort Pontchartrain and founded the city of Detroit.

2

The Hungry Men

*O*UT of a disastrous drop in the price of beaver had come one of the world's most significant cities. It was a long time before men realized what they had done, and the new concept of Michigan as a place to live, rather than as a resource to exploit, had to struggle hard for survival. The controls were in the hands of the exploiters, who felt that a rich, unspoiled country called for predators rather than settlers, and this idea was a long time dying. Nevertheless, Cadillac had sounded a new note, and it had a certain resonance.

Cadillac himself was eloquent. He built his fort, and houses near it for traders and workers; he cleared ground and raised French wheat and Indian corn—noting proudly that the latter stood eight feet tall; real corn-belt corn, if he had known it—and he made gardens, developed vineyards, and set out fruit trees, and looked about him and saw that it was good. In a report for the King's ministers he told about it:

"This country, so temperate, so fertile, and so beautiful that it may justly be called the earthly paradise of North America, deserves all the care of the King to keep it up to attract inhabitants to it, so that a solid settlement may be formed there which shall not be liable to the usual vicissitudes of the other posts in which only a mere garrison is placed." [1] He enlarged upon the

---

1. George May and Herbert Brinks, editors, *A Michigan Reader, 11,000 B.C. to A.D. 1865* (Grand Rapids: Eerdmans Publishing Co., 1974), p. 82.

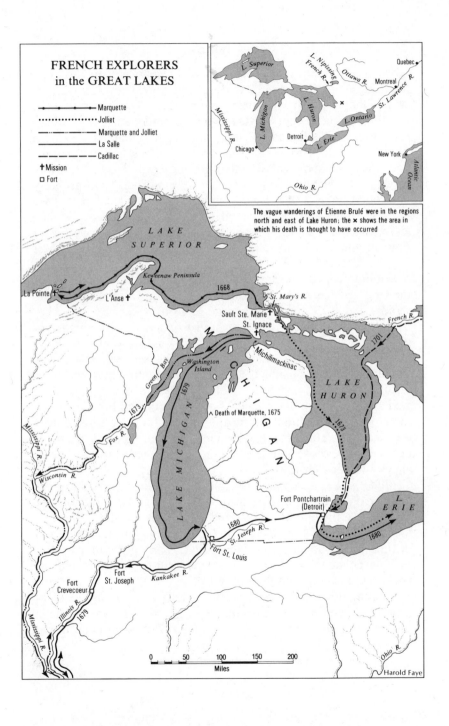

FRENCH EXPLORERS
in the GREAT LAKES

- •——•——• Marquette
- •••••••••• Jolliet
- —•—•—•— Marquette and Jolliet
- ————— La Salle
- — — — — Cadillac
- † Mission
- □ Fort

The vague wanderings of Étienne Brulé were in the regions north and east of Lake Huron; the ✕ shows the area in which his death is thought to have occurred

L. Superior
L. Nipissing
French R.
Ottawa R.
Quebec
Montreal
St. Lawrence R.
L. Michigan
L. Huron
L. Ontario
Detroit
L. Erie
New York
Mississippi R.
Chicago
Ohio R.
Atlantic Ocean

LAKE SUPERIOR

Keweenaw Peninsula

1668

La Pointe †

L'Anse †

St. Mary's R.

Sault Ste. Marie †
St. Ignace †

French R.

1701

Michilimackinac

1673

Green Bay

Washington Island

1679

LAKE MICHIGAN

LAKE HURON

1673

△ Death of Marquette, 1675

1673

Fox R.

Mississippi R.

Wisconsin R.

Fort Pontchartrain
(Detroit)

L. ERIE

1680

1680

St. Joseph R.

Fort St. Louis

Fort St. Joseph

Kankakee R.

Fort Crevecoeur

Illinois R.

1679

Mississippi R.

Ohio R.

| 0 | 50 | 100 | 150 | 200 |

Miles

Harold Faye

advantages, pointing out that most of the Indians who had clustered about Michilimackinac were now living around Detroit,
where they brought in large quantities of good furs—taken,
mostly, within a short distance of the settlement—and where
they were not debased by the brandy given them by lawless
woods runners. The woods runners themselves, for that matter,
had vanished somewhere, into thin air or into some faraway
forest, and the trade carried on here was all legal and properly
controlled. "It is the Lord's vine," Cadillac declared; "we
must let it be cultivated by all sorts of good laborers." [2] To
show that he was in earnest, he brought his wife over from
France, and so did his chief lieutenant, and these were the first
European women to live in Michigan.

Cadillac called the new settlement *La Ville d'Étroit,* city of
the strait, just as *La Ville de Sault Ste. Marie* was the city of the
rapids; and, in time, one became Detroit, while the other became the Soo; and when the English came in, the names remained unchanged. As it happened, the English wanted to come
in on the undefended southland before the new settlement was
founded, and they planned to bring the Iroquois in with them.
Cadillac acted just in time; with this fort in position, the in-
vasion did not take place, and Michigan remained French for six
more decades. Cadillac got meager thanks for his efforts. Planting and cultivating the Lord's vine, he had stepped on some
very sensitive toes, and after a time he was called to Quebec to
answer various charges. In the end, the charges collapsed, and
Cadillac was restored to duty, but he had done what the commander of an outpost must never do: he had Made Trouble for
the Home Office; and in 1710, the authorities transferred him all
the way down to Louisiana. Michigan knew him no more, and
in time forgot about him—except that, many generations later,
as if in belated recompense, a swanky automobile adopted his
name and made a household word of it.

Looking down the immeasurable years, we see Cadillac's Detroit as a beguiling showcase model of a town, unreal, not made
for anyone to *live* in, resembling modern Detroit in nothing but

2. May and Brinks, *A Michigan Reader,* p. 85.

the great river flowing past. Its streets were narrow, ten or fifteen feet wide for the most part; the houses were incredibly
small, perched on lots that averaged twenty feet wide by
twenty-five feet deep, and most of them were made of squared
logs with slab roofs. Some of them appear to have had no stoves
or fireplaces whatever, and there must have been communal
kitchens so that people who lived in these chilly boxes could
cook their food. The whole place was surrounded by a log palisade, and there was a strict rule that everyone must come inside
the gates at night. Some of the inhabitants did have farms outside the palisade, and the surrounding Indians were friendly
enough, but they were notoriously light-fingered, and anyone
who stayed outside with farm tools or reaped crops was apt to
lose his possessions overnight—and anyway, in this country, no
settler took very many chances, even with friendly Indians.

Inside the palisade, there were many gardens; each soldier in
the garrison was allotted half an acre and was required to cultivate it. The settlement contained a church, a barn, and a warehouse, and the river yielded a great many fish. Salt was expensive, however—people did not yet realize that one of the
country's greatest deposits of salt lay not far underground—so
no fish were preserved for winter use or for export. There were
sailing craft along the waterfront, but they were small, open
boats, nothing like the mysteriously lost *Griffon*. Travel to
lower Canada still went by canoe along the Ottawa in the traditional way.

In 1713, the struggle we remember as Queen Anne's War
ended, which meant that France and England were again at
peace, as they sometimes were, sporadically and uneasily, for a
period of two centuries or more. It was time to look ahead to the
next war, because this last one had left the French under certain
handicaps. England now held the Hudson's Bay country and
could tap the lakes' fur trade from the north; she also held New-
foundland and Nova Scotia and might some day use her navy to
close the St. Lawrence, which would starve a French Canada
that could not feed itself. It was time to refortify the north country, as La Salle had urged; time also to open up some farms
after Cadillac's pattern, so that everybody could be fed. The

damage done by the withdrawal caused by the ruinous surfeit of prime beaver pelts must be made good.

Michilimackinac came first, both Fort de Buade and Mission St. Ignace having been destroyed when soldiers and traders were called away. A French inspector who went up there shortly before Cadillac was transferred to Louisiana reported that the settlement was still occupied by a baker's dozen of woods runners, who got along happily without protection; they smuggled in brandy, traded it for furs, and got the furs to Montreal by hiring Indians to transport them, the Indians posing as independent operators. This example was alluring to those who did not like restraint; and by 1712, Michilimackinac held forty or fifty men, with a great many Indians living not far away. It was time for the King's servants to re-assert control; and in 1715, Fort Michilimackinac was re-established. It was not put where the old fort had been but was built south of the strait, and as soon as it was properly manned, the Lake Superior trade, abandoned when Cadillac concentrated operations at Detroit, was reopened. At about the same time, an expedition followed La Salle's old trail up the St. Joseph River, far to the south, planting a fort and a mission near the site of the portage to the Kankakee—where the city of Niles is today.

So the French tightened their grip, as they supposed, and eventually there were log-and-dirt forts in a long curve through the wilderness to the south, from the Illinois country all the way to the Allegheny River and Lake Erie. Now the lakes country was secure, if military measures could make it so.

They could not. Cadillac had seen it; if the French wanted to hold this country, they had to occupy it. New France needed a stronger base than the King's soldiers and ships could provide by themselves; it would inevitably be lost unless it produced something more nourishing than the skins of wild animals. Already, far to the east, English colonists were venturing over the mountains, irresistibly drawn by the most powerful lure ever presented to civilized man: the lure of rich, open, empty land, enough for thousands and tens of thousands of men, each one of whom by getting his share of it could have a freedom such as no common man in Europe had ever hoped for. If the French would not use this land, these men would most certainly take it away from them.

At which point it is necessary to emphasize that this open, empty land was already being used and was not in the least empty. It was occupied by the Indians, who had been living there for a great many centuries, and by their standards it already held all of the people it could support. Aside from the fact that men of any time who see great riches lying on a weaker person's land are all too likely to go and take those riches by force, devising suitable rationalizations afterward, the European of that day simply was not fitted to understand that the Indian actually was using this land. The Indian's towns were few, small, and far apart; some of them were hardly more than temporary camps, and the patches where he raised his corn and beans and pumpkins were not big; it was almost inevitable that the man from Europe, seeing all of this, would conclude that the Indian was ignorant, shiftless, and improvident and had no rightful claim to this land. But the very nature of the Indian's society meant that it needed vast tracts of untamed land. The Indian had to hunt to fill out his diet and to get the skins with which he made his clothing; more recently, he had become obliged to hunt much more intensively than ever to buy the tools, weapons, and other goods that the trader had for sale. A settled, cultivated country was one in which Indian culture could not survive. None of this was clear to the white man, especially to the land-hungry white who was peering over the Alleghenies, already convinced that the Indian was a bloodthirsty savage whose culture ought not to survive.

These land-hungry whites, the English colonists, would assuredly come in if they were not stopped, and so the French strengthened their defenses. Not long after Cadillac left, the Fox Indians—one Great Lakes tribe that never warmed up to the French—tried to capture Detroit, supposedly egged on by British agents; the Indians who lived near the settlement made common cause with the French and drove them away, killing nearly a thousand of them and leading various French officials to mutter that the whole tribe ought to be wiped out. Nothing came of this. The Foxes took refuge in Wisconsin, and their antagonism to white interlopers surfaced more than a century later in Black Hawk's War, the last Indian fight in the whole lakes area.

So the high country seemed to be secure, and perhaps what it needed was a firm hand in defense; Cadillac might have been wrong in calling the country an earthly paradise for farmers, but it was clearly an earthly paradise for beaver, marten, mink, otter, and similar creatures, and if the military cordon could be sustained, this land might be held just as it was, frozen in time, a wilderness that retained its virginity even while it was being violently ravaged. Despite the surpluses that had been so bothersome a few years earlier, the fur trade still made men rich. It provided so many things France needed: material for hats, caps, gloves, robes, collars, coats, cloaks, and so on, through a long list, and if beaver remained the most valuable, the lowly muskrat led all animals in numbers taken. Furthermore, despite their best efforts, the traders had not yet appreciably diminished the available supply.

It was inevitable that the French effort to hold this country should fail, because, from first to last, the basic idea was to enrich France—or a few important Frenchmen, at any rate—rather than to plant and nourish a successful colony. The men who directed the affairs of New France wanted to set up outposts for traders, rather than permanent communities, and the active agents—the woods runners, the men who had escaped from the law and from civilization and had stepped blithely out of Europe into the old Stone Age—wanted to get away from organized society, rather than to nourish it. They had been all over the new land; wherever an explorer found a new waterway or an official saw a place for a new fort or settlement, the woods runners had been there first. These men might huddle around such trading posts as Michilimackinac or the Soo while they rested, got fresh supplies, and in general caught their breath, but the last thing they wanted was to see farmsteads, towns, and highways there. The very officials who were supposed to see to it that the country was properly developed did not have their hearts in it at all; they could run the trade the way they wanted to, no matter what the King's writ might say, so long as nobody but traders and woods runners came and went; but in a settled country, their style would be cramped. To make matters worse, it appeared that the new settlers were likely to be Normans, known as obstreperous people, prone to find fault with their governors even back in France.

In spite of all this, settlement did increase—very slowly, but perceptibly. The clustered huts around such places as Michili-mackinac and the Soo began to look less like roosting places for the homeless and more like actual towns, as some of the men who had come so far to get away from civilization edged back into it, marrying Indian girls with due formality and squaring away as sober householders. At the Fort of St. Joseph, far down by the Kankakee portage, soldiers brought their wives, and presently the parish register was recording the births of white children, the first in all of Michigan. By 1750, some fifty families were living there, and enthusiastic reports were coming in. One man said the country along the St. Joseph river grew "the finest vines in the world" and was "the richest district in all that country," while a priest at the mission wrote of it as "this earthly paradise." [3] Their enthusiasm is understandable; they were in what is now Berrien County, southern anchor to the famous Lake Michigan fruit belt and still a notable land of vine-yards.

At about this time, the French government at last made a real effort to stimulate immigration to Detroit; a man who agreed to go there and stay would be given a cow, a pig, various farm implements, even a wagon, along with a grant of land. People began to respond, and soon the west bank of the Detroit River was striped with the farms of the *habitants*. (The term *habitant* was insisted on, and borne proudly: it meant that a man was a step above a peasant.) These farms were laid out in the style al-ready typical of French Canada, where there were hardly any roads, and travel went by water; they were two or three hundred feet wide and a mile long, so that each one could front on the river, and also so that each farm family could have near neigh-bors. On wash days, the *habitants'* wives took soiled clothing

3. Milo Quaife, *Lake Michigan* (Indianapolis and New York: Bobbs-Merrill Co., Inc., 1948), p. 53.

down to the river, soaked the garments, and then laid them on the stones and pounded them with wooden mallets, the chonk-chonk sounding pleasantly all along the water front, with a bubble of neighborly talk riding over it.

The cramped, incomplete Detroit of Cadillac's day had developed marvelously. Some roving soul had touched the edge of Michigan's unbroken pineries, seeing the fringe of the vast forests of unimaginable trees, deep shade, magical shadows, and the implicit peace of God; finding this on the edge of the Thumb country near the St. Clair River, trees that were breathtakingly majestic and at the same time immediately useful. A sawmill, first of many, was built there, and sawn lumber was brought down to the city of the strait, and now not all of Detroit's houses were made of squared logs. They were built more spaciously, some of them, two stories high in many cases, and there were cedar shingles to put on the roofs. There were quarries not far away; lime kilns had been put into operation; proper foundations could be laid for new houses, and some could even be built of stone. The *habitants'* houses ceased to be mere shelters from the wind and cold and took on grace and ease; still made of squared-off logs, for the most part, but laid out with huge central fireplaces and given four rooms on the ground floor—parlor, dining room, sleeping room, and kitchen, with a loft overhead and sometimes with dormer windows in the roof. City and country folk alike had horses, scrubby little beasts, to be sure, but they made all the difference; and if there were hardly any roads, the rivers were frozen all winter long, and *habitants* and townsfolk alike hitched horses to sleighs and drove gaily along the Detroit River and downstream to another waterway, a marvelously peaceful rural stream known as River Rouge. Food was plentiful, and the French had something of a talent for having a good time together. During the long winter months, the town was closed down, the outside world as far away as if it existed on another planet; but this was part of the natural order of things, and nobody minded. There was a *town* here, with snug houses and warm fires and companionship, priests and doctors and such technicians as people needed in those days, and the cold, heavy shadow of the wilderness had been pushed back, so that people could relax, toast their toes by the fire, and sleep well at night.

An enormous change had begun to take place, if anyone had bothered to notice it. The likes of Étienne Brulé were meeting final defeat. In this town, clinging confidently but tenuously to the edge of great night, a new attitude had developed, new at least to this part of the world. The wilderness now looked like an enemy. It was something to be conquered, tamed, beaten into submission, animals killed and trees cut down—and red Indians defanged, given hoes in place of tomahawks, turned into imitation white men, their dreams bleached and faded and robbed of all power to move men. There was going to be light in the forest ("Daylight in the swamps!" the lumber-camp foremen of a later day would yell profanely, calling the men with axes to work, meaning the same thing the French in Detroit were beginning without realizing it to mean in every act and every step), and in this light could be seen towns and highways and shops and farms and all of the other things that would set men free at the same time they bound them in new chains.

The country had always held riches, of course, but the real magnet that drew men here had been that it offered escape; here, at the least, a man was not forced into a mold, his life constricted by the nearness and the prejudices of innumerable neighbors, and if he wanted to he could move out to the realm of the wholly lawless and live as he chose—with, to be sure, the penalty of swift death if he chose unwisely. Here, in fine, was absolute freedom, and no European had been offered anything like this before. Now the towns were going to spring up, and although they too might offer freedom, it would lead inevitably toward the old conformity. Brulé's enchanted path was vanishing, because the country it crossed was going to be transformed and because no ordered society could be built out of men who had abandoned all restraints. No woods runner ever made a clearing, laid out a farm, and squatted there to raise a family, and the people in Detroit understood this perfectly. Yet the profound and subtle lure of the wilderness remained to touch the restless dreams of the people in Detroit and their descendants down to the present generation. The wilderness is always an enemy to be beaten, but it always exercises a fascination. The Wild West evokes an instinctive response, and it had its first incarnation, not on the sagebrush plains, but in the land of blowing trees, unbroken shade, and the huge lakes that lay empty beyond the horizon.

But the wilderness had not yet been beaten, and although Detroit presently had eighty buildings and fifteen hundred white inhabitants, counting the farmers who lived outside the village, the process was going much too slowly. New France contained sixty thousand whites, almost all of them living along the lower St. Lawrence, and in effect it was keeping an unlimited game preserve within arm's reach of two million English colonists who cared hardly at all about the game but were desperately hungry to possess the land the game lived on. The government in London, which supposedly controlled these hungry colonists, liked the idea of a big game preserve as well as the French did, but it held that the oligarchy enriched thereby ought to be English, rather than French; and in any case, it had an old score to settle with the French, and it perceived that it now had the muscle to settle it. The new war began in 1755.

Commander of French troops in New France was the Marquis de Montcalm, who saw disaster dead ahead. The British, he knew, could get the western country simply by seizing Quebec; take and keep the central stronghold, and the outland of little wooden forts would fall by itself, since it was by no means ready to stand on its own feet. But Montcalm found it completely impossible to get properly ready for the shock. He wanted to mobilize the army's reserves, to lay up proper stores of food, to check the general corruption that hampered all military efforts, and to break up the black market that drained away supplies; he could not, because the governor of Canada, the Marquis de Vaudreuil, was of the old school and would stand no interference with the status quo. Despairingly, Montcalm wrote to Paris, predicting defeat and complaining: "Our government is worthless. . . . Everybody appears to be in a hurry to make his fortune before the colony is lost." [4]

4. Russell McKee, *Great Lakes Country* (New York: Thomas Y. Crowell, 1966), p. 137.

Except at the one vital spot, the French defenses were good enough. Fort Duquesne had been built at the forks of the Ohio to prevent incursion to the Ohio country, and when British General Braddock marched into the wilderness, parade-ground style, to fight a parade-ground battle, the French and Indians were waiting for him, and Braddock lost his life, his army, and every shred of his reputation. A British attack on Fort Ticonderoga was beaten back, with two thousand redcoats shot down, and briefly things looked good for the French.

Very briefly. A better man marched on Fort Duquesne and took it, and Sir Jeffrey Amherst led an army that drove the French out of Ticonderoga and Crown Point. Then Wolfe came up the St. Lawrence to Quebec and climaxed what looked like a losing siege by slipping upstream, making a landing at night, and striking Montcalm's army in the open Plains of Abraham. Montcalm was killed, Wolfe was killed, the French army was routed, and the British had Quebec; and in the following year, another British army took Montreal, and lower Canada was gone. The same Marquis de Vaudreuil who had refused to rise to Montcalm's appeals now found himself making formal surrender of all of Canada. Men who had never seen the Great Lakes had won them for Great Britain; Michigan, which had seen none of the fighting, learned presently that it had been conquered, and that it must hoist a new flag and swear allegiance to a different king.

Probably that is not the best way to say it. Michigan then consisted very largely of Indians, with a few French soldiers, settlers, and traders for top-dressing, and most of the Indians knew of this war no more than what woods rumors had told them. Some of the Ottawas had gone east to help defeat Braddock before Fort Duquesne, and they came back with a low opinion of the British, considering them poor soldiers and panicky, who did not know how to fight in the woods and did not seem to have much stomach for it in any case. These Indians did not feel conquered; they got along well with the French, taking one thing with another, and a good many of the traders and woods runners were quietly telling them to sit tight—the French king had gone to sleep, but he would wake up after a while, and everything would go on as it had been.

Reality came in, finally, in November of 1760. There had been a week of dull rain, but at last the weather cleared, and there was still autumn color on the woods when a flotilla of whaleboats started up the Detroit River from Lake Erie, headed for Detroit, oars dipping rhythmically, the cross of St. George on the red flags that fluttered overhead. In the boats were two hundred of the toughest Indian-fighters in all America, Rogers' Rangers, men who dressed like frontiersmen, carried rifles like white soldiers and tomahawks like Indians, and believed that they could go any place an Indian could go and whip anybody they found there. With them, commanding, was Major Robert Rogers himself, who had created these Rangers and led them in action and who was come now to add his own few sentences to the legends of the state that would some day exist here.

Major Rogers at that moment was of fabulous fame. New Englanders who had lived desperately on exposed farms and villages under the overhang of the dark Canadian forest, from which red raiders with fire arrows and scalping knives could strike without warning and then fade back into the dreadful shadows, had safety and contentment now; Rogers and his Rangers in one daring stroke had smashed the St. Francis Indians and ended such raids forever. Amherst knew Rogers as the man who understood wilderness warfare as no other English or provincial soldier did, and when the French surrendered and it was time to send men into the deepest wilderness of all, to take possession for the British crown, Amherst sent Rogers as a matter of course.

So now Rogers's flotilla rowed up abreast of the settlement, ran its whaleboats on the beach on what is now the Ontario side of the river, and sent two officers and a corporal's guard over with a message for the French commandant of Fort Pontchartrain, who thus got formal notification from his superiors that all had been lost and an equally formal note from Major Rogers, telling him to strike his flag and lay down his arms.

It was gaudy to look at. Hundreds of Indians, painted like Joseph's coat, men who enjoyed a good spectacle as well as any people alive, were massed on the long slope that led down to the river; the fleur-de-lis came down the flagpole, and the British flag went up. French regulars marched out and stacked arms, followed by the Canadian militia—and then it was all over, and the Indians raised a great shout when the Rangers occupied Fort Pontchartrain. Rogers arranged to send the French regulars down to lower Canada, where they could take ship for France, and he told the *habitants* and artisans who made up the militia that they could remain on their farms or in their shops if they would swear allegiance to King George. This they promptly did, no other course being open to them. The Indians were highly impressed by this display of power, but one thing did puzzle them: why, having disarmed all of these prisoners, did the British not put the whole lot to death?

The plan was for Rogers to go on up Lake Huron to the Straits and then take possession of Michilimackinac, Green Bay, and St. Joseph, not to mention the Soo: this done, British control of the Great Lakes would be complete, and all of the Michigan country would be secure. Lake Huron is a bad lake to travel on, late in November, however, especially for men who have to go in open boats, and storms and ice were too much. Rogers gave up and returned to Detroit for the winter. In the spring, he would go on and assert British control over Lake Michigan and Lake Superior, and in the end it was done so. By the fall of 1761, the formalities were finished; and for whatever it might be worth to him, King George now owned Michigan.

It would not actually be worth very much because, of all the bits of empire the British crown acquired, this one had the shortest life: the king had title to it for twenty-two years and held it irregularly by force of bureaucratic stubbornness for six or seven years longer, and then he lost it because of the incredible ineptitude of his agents and the flaming determination of his far-off subjects to be their own men; and much good it ever did him while he held it. But for the moment, he did have title to it; and the interesting question is, simply: What had he got?

He had got two peninsulas of land, some of it gnarled and craggy and some of it rich with rolling hills and deep green forests and occasional prairie plots of unused fertility—all of it beautiful beyond any measure known to the new owners. The two peninsulas were rich, rich beyond calculation, full of a wealth that eighteenth-century eyes simply could not measure: mile upon mile of forests, veins of copper worth more in hard money than all of the sums the crown ever spent in the new world, deposits of iron whose time had not yet come, fisheries and salt wells, and bubbling, underground oceans of chemicals-in-water that would some day support industries of a kind not dreamed of in 1763. A great deal of this wealth was not of the kind men then could see, even when they looked hard. It was all so very far away. The Keweenaw Peninsula did indeed hold copper—typically, the copper had been discovered by missionaries who had taken the vow of poverty, not by the money-grubbers who had gone straight by without seeing what lay under their feet—and besides, Lake Superior was more remote from the world's markets in that time than any place on earth can be today. (How would you get copper ore from the north country to the European smelters, in the late eighteenth century? By birchbark canoe?)

When the king's agents looked at Michigan, all they could see was the animals whose skins were adorned with valuable fur. It was natural for men to see these, because these animals were the real reason why white men had wanted to come to Michigan in the first place. The tragic mistake the British made was that, when they looked at Michigan, they could not ever see the Indians.

There were perhaps ten thousand Indians here then, and you can study the names of the tribes until your face is blue without adding much to your knowledge, because, essentially, they were all much the same people: Chippewas, (or Ojibways, Outchibous, Otchipwe, or what you choose) and Ottawas, and the blend of Potawatomis, Fox, Sauk, and Massauaketon that are often lumped together as the People of the Fire; the Miamis, sometimes called the Omaumeg; and the remnants of the Hurons, driven from their Georgian Bay homeland by the cruel Iroquois, to whose family they once belonged, given now to living about Detroit, known of late as the Wyandot.

These tribes had individual ways of life that rested on a common base, and the differences seemed to reflect mostly the varying geographical restrictions and possibilities in the areas where they lived. Thus the Chippewas, most northerly of the lot, lived beyond the country in which men could profitably plant seeds and harvest crops, indeed lived mostly where planting and reaping could not be done at all; so they were hunters and fishers and inevitably wanderers who could not live in fixed villages and whose cultural level was conditioned by that fact. They swapped skins and meat to the Ottawas, who lived to the south of them, in return for corn and beans the Ottawas had raised. The Ottawas, in turn, had regular villages near their farms, but went en masse to fishing camps in the summer, and in winter sent men into the deep woods to hunt because farming by itself could not support them. They had things better than the Chippewas did, but, like them, they needed a great deal of elbow room for survival. Incidentally, their dealings with the Chippewas had made inveterate traders of both tribes, and from the first they liked to do business with the woods runners and licensed traders from lower Canada.

The Fire People, still farther south, lived much as the Ottawas did, except that the climate was milder and the soil richer in their country, so they could stay at home more, and their villages could be a little closer together. They were still widely scattered, by the white men's standards. Luckiest of all were the tribes who lived in the southernmost part of the lower peninsula, like the Miamis; here, the soil not only yielded good crops, but also supported so much game that the Indians could do their hunting in the immediate neighborhood of their towns. The Hurons, refugees in this land, seemed to accommodate themselves most easily to the white man's settlements, and Cadillac had had no trouble persuading them to come down to the Detroit River from the less hospitable north.

Thus the Indians distributed themselves very much as the whites who dispossessed them did later, with many people living in the productive regions and few living in the hardscrabble country. Strikingly enough, the relative densities of population in the different parts of Michigan are today just about what they were when no one but Indians lived here. Which proves, possibly, that, after all, the land molds people to its own measure, either in the age of chipped stone or in the age of Madison Ave-

nue tempered by nuclear fission; and it may be that we are not
entirely the masters of our fate.

In any case, here were the Indians, the central fact in a place
where all the rules seemed to be off. The French had understood
them, but the men in Paris had decreed that whatever was done
here would be done only in order to make a profit; the British
were equally insistent on a profit, but they did not even try to
understand the Indians, because the master race did not need to
understand the notions and emotions of mere natives; and in the
end the high country got away from both of them and followed
its own strange destiny, whose end is not yet apparent.

Montcalm had seen it, with his bitter cry that all anyone
wanted was a chance to make a fortune. He was in his grave
when Major Rogers came up the river, but he would have understood perfectly what the Major found when he got into Detroit. Tucked away safely in the warehouse, the Major discovered, were furs worth $500,000.

3

Stars and Stripes

T took the Indians very little time to discover that the British were not like the French. At such places as Michilimackinac, the French had regularly given ammunition and clothing to the tribesmen who lived nearby. This was an understood thing, a custom that had grown up over the years, not because the French were generous, but simply because it kept the Indians in good temper and made the bargaining for furs go smoothly. Now it developed that the British did not have this habit and did not propose to acquire it. When one outpost commander notified Amherst that the Indians were growing discontented because gifts were lacking, Amherst replied haughtily, compacting into one sentence the blind arrogance that loses empires:

"As to appropriating a particular sum to be laid out yearly to the warriors in presents, etc., that I can by no means agree to; nor can I think it necessary to give them any presents by way of *Bribes*, for if they do not behave properly they are to be punished." [1]

Thus for the first time the Indians of the high country met the keep-the-natives-in-their-place spirit in its full flowering. They had seen no trace of this in the French, who exploited them as

1. Francis Parkman, *The Conspiracy of Pontiac*, 2 vols. (Boston: Little, Brown and Company, 1901), I:181–182.

royally as the greediest fur-trader could have wished, but who seemed to like them as human beings. The Indians were as sensitive as anyone to the nuances of behavior, and they did not like the attitude they were meeting now.

It went beyond hurt feelings. For these north-country Indians, the matter of continued gifts had become something close to a matter of life or death. The simple fact was that the Indians had become almost entirely dependent on the white man. The Indian only seemed to be living in the Stone Age. He really was a part of eighteenth-century Europe; he was working for the white man every day of his life; he had become a professional hunter and trapper to such an extent that he could no longer live as he used to live. He had to have the white man's weapons and tools and clothing, because he had ceased to make his own; he would have been foolish to go on making them, because the white man's things were ever so much better than anything the Indian could produce—but the process had got the Indian into an infernal bind.

He was no longer independent, and although he tried desperately to cling to his old culture it had been cut loose from its roots. He made his living by killing and skinning animals, not for his own use, but in order to buy guns, knives, kettles, blankets, gewgaws of all kinds, and the most enticing and ruinous benefit of all, alcohol. He could eat the meat of many of the animals whose pelts he removed, but in many cases he no longer had the time to operate the farms that once supplemented his diet; he was likely to be getting corn, flour, wild rice, and other foodstuffs from the traders, who in turn bought them from tribes that were farming for the white man and not for themselves. The Indian supported and fed the white trader and depended on him for help in starving times, and the Indian absolutely had to have the gifts that the authorities at the settlements periodically distributed—exactly as the wage-earner of a much later date has to have the unemployment benefits that enable him to live at the mercy of an inscrutable mass-production society.

All of this meant much more than the sad fact that the sturdy son of the forest was no longer standing on his own feet; it

meant that profound changes were taking place in Indian life itself. The weight of the white man's presence was pressuring all
of these woodland people in the direction of the sort of culture
the Chippewas had evolved in the cold wilderness that offered
them nothing more than life at the subsistence level. The Chippewas had always existed as a hunting mechanism because in
their bleak homeland that was the price of survival; and this
kind of tribal life was exactly the kind that was ultimately called
for by the system of fur trading that the Europeans had introduced. The Indian was beginning to live in a new cultural at-
mosphere that he had not bargained for and in which he could
not be happy. His society was no longer primeval; it lived in the
shadow of a society richer, stronger, and infinitely more complex; and as the years went on, the Indian's society grew weaker
and duller.

The Indian may not have understood why things were hap-
pening to him, but he was beginning to see that his number was
up. The woods runners who visited all Indian camps liked the
British no more than the red men did, and they were circulating
ominous stories: far to the east, in what we now know as Pennsylvania, white settlers were filtering in and making farms, with
Fort Pitt at the forks of the Ohio to protect them, and if British
occupancy meant that in the east, would it not some day mean
the same thing here in Michigan? The Indians began to suspect
that it would, a suspicion abundantly justified by later events;
meanwhile, they listened to the wild preaching of a forest wan-
derer known rather vaguely as the Delaware Prophet, who was
calling them to repentance and reform.

The Prophet circulated mostly in the Ohio country, but he had
a voice that carried far. He appears to have been of defective
mental balance; he had trances in which great visions came to
him; he carried a scrap of birchbark with strange hieroglyphics
on it; he sought to purify himself by taking emetics frequently;
and when he talked, he was forever breaking into tears. He had
had some sort of instruction in Christianity, apparently, which
gave a strange evangelical tinge to his discourse, and he had
dedicated himself to the task of leading all the Indians to give
up the white man's ways, repent their indulgence in the white

man's sins, and go back to the life they had lived before the white man came. He was calling, in short, for complete nonintercourse between Indians and whites: humanly impossible, no doubt, but probably the only thing that could ever have saved the Indians from the slow disaster that was waiting for them.

Among those who heard him was a war chief of the Ottawas, a man named Pontiac, with whom the British were about to become much better acquainted.

Pontiac had led a war party to the fight in front of Fort Duquesne, where Braddock was overwhelmed, and he had come away with a poor opinion of the British. Sometime later, in 1760, when Major Rogers was bringing his flotilla westward along the Ohio shore of Lake Erie, Pontiac had called on him when the Rangers were in camp, waiting for stormy Lake Erie to grow calm. His purpose in calling was slightly shadowy; evidently, he wanted to make sure that Major Rogers, who was about to enter the Michigan country, understood that this was Pontiac's country and that Pontiac was to be treated with full respect. Rogers got the message. He understood Indians as his superiors never did, and the British might have saved a world of trouble if they had left matters in the high country in his hands. This they did not do—it must be admitted that Rogers had a genius for being hard to get along with—and after he had taken possession of the Lake Michigan forts in 1763, Rogers was sent back east. For the moment, however, he and Pontiac got along well enough.

As Rogers could have told them, the British authorities were driving straight for a costly showdown. In 1762, the commandant at Detroit, reflecting on the things he had been hearing about unrest in the deep forest and reflecting also on the fact that he was not supposed to distribute any more powder to the Indians, warned his superiors that the tribes were getting very restless, and added: "I assure you they only want a good opportunity to fall upon us if they had encouragement from an enemy." [2]

2. Howard Peckham, "Pontiac and the Indian Uprising," in May and Brinks, *A Michigan Reader*, p. 105.

The encouragement was forthcoming very soon. Although France had been compelled to surrender all of Canada, France and Great Britain were still at war; France held the Louisiana country (with Spain for an ally, now), and there was nothing in the surrender documents to say that France could not try to regain what had been lost. France was still an enemy, and French agents seem to have gone through the Ohio and Michigan country, calling the tribes to arms and assuring them that the French king would very soon recover the territory he had lost. Among those who listened was Pontiac, who in the end got credit for the whole uprising that resulted. He got credit for too much, and the flames that ran across the Ohio country were not of his doing. However, as he had told Rogers, he was top man in Michigan, and most of what happened here came straight from him.

One of the significant facts about Pontiac seems to have been that he was a man of great dignity. Montcalm had given him the uniform of a French officer, white with blue trimmings and much gold lace, and while Pontiac never wore this at ordinary times or while he was on the war path, he did put it on when some great occasion came; he was not the rum-soaked tinhorn chieftain of the type familiar in the west a century later, loafing about in stained regimentals to make a show for tourists, but a leader of men who understood his own worth and now and then dressed for the part. As a matter of fact, what the British never realized was that all Indians were men of dignity. Dignity was the one quality British dominance never allowed a native; and when all is said about it, the basic cause of the war that is remembered now as Pontiac's Conspiracy was the simple fact that the British did not like the Indians and let the Indians see that they did not. That same fatal inability to disguise their contempt for people they considered their inferiors—a broad category, all in all—was in the end to cost the British their American colonies.

Detroit was where the British were, chiefly, in Michigan, and so Detroit was where Pontiac went into action. In the spring of 1763, he convoked and harangued a meeting of warriors on the Ecorse River, a few miles southwest of Detroit.

It is important to remember that, although Pontiac was called a chief, he had no real authority. There was no Indian government in Michigan; each tribe was independent, so was each tribal band, and so was each individual Indian; no one had any power except what his own general status as a leader of men could give him. The Ottawas were Pontiac's people, but he could not order them to do anything whatever, and the other tribes were even further away from giving him automatic obedience. Indians would go to war if, individually, they thought it was a good idea; not otherwise. If he proposed to make war on the British, Pontiac had to be persuasive.

He was, in fact, very persuasive, greatly aided by the fact that throwing dead Englishmen into the Detroit River was an idea whose time had come, as far as most of the tribesmen were concerned. Calling for war, Pontiac declared that the French king (rousing from his costly sleep) had sent him a belt of wampum and had promised aid. He went on to say that the Delaware Prophet, meeting the Great Spirit in the world of visions beyond the horizon, had been warned that the Indians must give up the white man's ways and wipe out the white man himself. Pontiac got the response he wanted, and it remained only to make proper plans.

Clever strategy was called for, because, by Indian standards, the British stronghold was extremely powerful. The center of town, known as Fort Detroit, was enclosed by a log-and-dirt palisade, with bastions at the angles and blockhouses at the gates. It contained perhaps 100 houses, along with barracks for the 120-man garrison, whose numbers could be augmented by a scattering of militia—Canadians, mostly, who were not fond of the British, but who knew perfectly well that, if the Indians took the place by storm, they would probably kill everybody in it; the militia could be counted on for a sturdy defense.

Indian warriors were as brave as any, but they had no use for a headlong assault on a strong fort. They simply did not think that such fighting made any sense, and it may be that the two thousand red coats who had been shot down in the doomed assault on Fort Ticonderoga would have agreed with them. To take Detroit, the Indians would need to use deception, and Pontiac worked out a good trick.

He would lead forty picked men up to the gates of the fort and announce that they wanted to come in and smoke the calumet of peace, just to show they meant well. Once inside, with weapons hidden under their blankets, the Indians would wait until the British seemed properly relaxed; then they would bring out the weapons, emit war whoops and start killing people, throwing the gates open so that the tribesmen outside could come in and help. In short order, the entire garrison would be destroyed. The idea seemed good, and plans were made accordingly.

As so often happens, however, there was a bad security leak. To this day, no one is quite certain what happened; there are several versions, and the reader can take his choice. Most romantic is the tale that a beautiful Indian maiden (a princess, beyond doubt, because the beautiful Indian maiden in such cases is always a princess, even though that rank did not exist among the Indians) had fallen in love with Major Gladwin, the British commandant, learned what was up, slipped into the fort, and told him. By another story, it was a friendly Ottawa warrior who gave the game away; by still another, a British soldier who had cultivated inter-racial harmony so effectively that he had been adopted into an Indian family got warning from his sister. It is also said that a Canadian woman, chancing to visit an Ottawa village, saw various braves who had cut down the barrels of their muskets so that the weapons were less than a yard long, which probably marks the first appearance in American history of the sawed-off shotgun. A local blacksmith, hearing this story, recalled that for several days Indians had been trying to borrow files and hacksaws from him for some undisclosed but probably nefarious purpose; and all of this, it is said, got back to headquarters, where it made the authorities properly suspicious. The gun barrels were cut down, of course, so that the weapons could be hidden under blankets.

Whatever happened, Gladwin was on the alert, and when Pontiac and his braves went in for the pipe-of-peace ceremony, all of the soldiers were on duty, ready to shoot; there were extra guards at the gates, which were swung shut as soon as Pontiac's party entered, and Major Gladwin and his officers were wearing swords and pistols, giving Pontiac a correct but very frosty reception. The peace pipe got smoked, but the harmony it was supposed to evoke was invisible, and when Pontiac led his men out afterward he was an extremely wrathful Indian.

He remained wrathful for two or three days, while the fort's garrison remained on duty, with officers on the ramparts day and night, and after dark there was a great throbbing of war drums in the Indian camps, along with wild outbursts of yelling; and at last there was actual shooting, with Pontiac's men taking long-range shots at the palisades and the soldiers shooting long-range in response, with neither side getting serious injury. The Indians rampaged all up and down the range of houses and farms along the river, and a couple of English residents caught there were speedily slain. The Indians did not consider the French settlers enemies, and the French, being altogether at their mercy, did nothing to make them change their point of view.

It settled down, then, to a siege, a type of warfare that Indian tradition did not allow for; and perhaps the best measure of Pontiac's ability as a war leader is the fact that he held his lines in position for several months. To take the fort by storm was out of the question, but he did come fairly close to starving it into submission. Only fairly close, all things considered, because this fight was for table stakes, winner take all, and the British would never have surrendered, because they knew that the victors would infallibly butcher every last one of them. They held on, and the horizon grew very dark. Indian war parties swept all across the Ohio country, overwhelming forts from Sandusky to the Maumee and the Wabash; Fort Pitt itself was in danger, and in all of Michigan everything but Detroit was gone. St. Joseph had been taken; by ill fortune the fort at the Soo had been destroyed by accidental fire just before the war broke out, and—worst of all—Michilimackinac had been taken and most of its garrison had been killed.

The kind of trickery that failed at Detroit had worked at Michilimackinac. There had been no security leaks here, and to the last moment the British were serene and unsuspecting. On June 4, birthday of King George and so a day for general relaxation, there was a great game of lacrosse on the level ground just outside the main gate of the fort. Indian women clustered all around, wrapped in blankets, watching with stolid interest; British officers looked on, laughing, calling out to make bets on one side or the other. The tide of play surged up and down the field, and finally one player gave a mighty swipe with his racket and sent the ball flying inside the fort. The players ran in after it, shouting and shouldering one another, the British officers got a final chuckle out of the mad scramble—and then the Indian women drew tomahawks from under their blankets and handed them to the stripped-down braves, and all at once the idling British were mercilessly cut down.

The Michilimackinac business was slightly odd. This country belonged to the Chippewas and the Ottawas, Chippewas on the Lake Huron side, Ottawas along Lake Michigan; the principal Chippewa settlements were on Mackinac and Bois Blanc Islands, while the Ottawas lived mostly at a village the French had rendered as L'Arbre Croche, the Crooked Tree, several miles southwest of the fort in the lee of a long sandy peninsula known as Waugoshance Point. Pontiac was an Ottawa, but his appeal for all-out war had been heeded by the Chippewas rather than by his own people, and it was the Chippewas who seized the fort and killed most of its occupants. The Ottawas came around later, offended because the Chippewas had acted without them, and demanded a settlement; part of the loot was handed over to them, along with the commandant of the fort, Major Etherington, another officer, and eleven private soldiers. A fur trader named Alexander Henry also escaped alive, and later he wrote a graphic account of the whole business. He was a close friend of an Ottawa brave, who ransomed him and took him off to safety in the upper peninsula.

Small matters could make the difference between life and death, in the north country of that time. One small thing was that the Ottawa leader, Chief Wawatam, had less blood lust than most of the Chippewas—the Ottawas generally tended to be milder than those primitive hunters—so he refused to kill his prisoners. While the Chippewas were killing and eating their own captives, the Ottawas got theirs off to L'Arbre Croche and kept them alive. Another small thing was the accidental presence, just at that time, near the British outpost at Green Bay, of a party of Sioux Indians, who had checked in to confer with the local commandant and who were there when news of the Michilimackinac massacre came in. The Sioux were periodically and bitterly at war with the Chippewas for possession of the country around the west end of Lake Superior, and when the local tribesmen around Green Bay began to talk about storming the British fort there—it was pitifully weak, manned by just eighteen soldiers—the Sioux intervened. If the Chippewas were leading this fight on the British, they themselves were on the British side, and if necessary would fight for them.

In the end, after long negotiations, a deal was made. The British abandoned the Green Bay fort—considering their small numbers and the fact that Michilimackinac was gone, and maybe Detroit, too, for all they knew, there was nothing else they could do—and the Indians escorted them up to L'Arbre Croche, where they joined Major Etherington and his handful of troops. After more palavering, the united party got canoes, paddled up past the Straits, with Ottawas for protection, and at last went on down to Montreal by the old Ottawa River route. It had been a near thing. The Ottawas were not in the least enthusiastic about sending them back to lower Canada, and their momentary air of tolerance might switch to homicidal enmity at any moment. What restrained them was partly a feeling that the Chippewas had put one over, partly Chief Wawatam, and partly the influence of Father Jonois, who ran the Jesuit mission at L'Arbre Croche and preached moderation.

The siege of Detroit went on and on. British reinforcements from the east tried to come up the river from Lake Erie, compiled tales of high adventure to enthrall posterity, and accomplished little. A stronger expedition, late in July, brought 280 soldiers and some badly needed rations to the fort, encouraging everybody so much that an infantry battalion presently marched out, in an unsophisticated effort to take Pontiac by surprise. This could not be done; Pontiac's braves were watchful, drove the party back with heavy loss, and the innocent little creek where the battle was fought is known to this day as

Bloody Run. Pontiac's people bragged that they had won a great victory.

But the stars in their courses were set against them. The British who came in from the east brought something more than the muscle for a Braddock-type offensive; they brought official word that France and Britain had made peace, which meant that whatever Pontiac did now must be done strictly on his own. This was decisive, and everybody knew it, and before long the Wyandots and Potawatomis sent in delegations and made peace. For a while, Pontiac held the rest in line; but in the fall, he got a message from the French commandant in the northern Louisiana country, to whom he had appealed for help: there could be no help, now or ever, because beyond the seas the incomprehensible white kings had made peace.

Then fall turned into winter, which ended everything. In the very nature of things, Pontiac could not have a year-round commissariat. When cold weather came, the tribes had to break up, so that the warriors could scatter to their winter hunting grounds. Once they scattered, they could not be reassembled. In the Ohio country, the story was the same: like Pontiac, the Indian leaders there had to admit that, without French help, the war could not be renewed. It was over. Pontiac tried hard to talk up a renewal of the fight, failed, and then faded out of history.

It had been close, and the British had had a fine scare, one result of which was that the formidable Major Rogers was sent out to take command at a restored Fort Michilimackinac. Rogers, who was always impatient of restraint, tried to set up a system by which the entire fur country from the Straits on, everything that was beyond Detroit's immediate reach, would be out from under everybody's control except that of the government at London, with whom the officer at Michilimackinac (Major Rogers, to be sure) would deal directly. He convened a great concourse of Indian leaders, smoked innumerable pipes of peace, promised to protect them from all white interlopers, and said that the trade goods they wanted would be taken to their most remote villages by his teams working out of Michilimackinac. This made sense to the Indians, but not to Rogers's superiors, who believed that he was trying to set up his own empire and suspected that he would wind up by making some sort of deal with France or Spain. Rogers was recalled and was accused of high crimes; brought to trial, he was acquitted, but his career was in fragments. The high country saw him no more. Like Pontiac, he faded out of history.

Yet Rogers may have been the last chance. The Indian country—Ohio Valley, Great Lakes Basin, Illinois country, everything west—had to be kept inviolate, by his scheme or some other, if the road to empire in America was to remain usable. Building this empire, Britain had taken on two problems that made a poisonous combination.

First, there was this Indian country, valuable as a source of furs, troublesome in that its native inhabitants, restless people given to violent action, must at the same time be exploited and protected, kept properly subservient but also somehow assuaged and made friendly. (Pontiac had served notice that the price of failure could be very high.) Second, there were the colonists along the Atlantic seaboard, who still talked like Englishmen but who were beginning to act more and more like Americans.

These people had stumbled on a most intoxicating bit of knowledge: that men could assert and enjoy unlimited freedom if they once got access to unlimited land. At bottom, European society in the eighteenth century was an intensely rural civilization. Everything was based on land; the whole structure of cities, banks, shops, corporations for trade and investment, haughty aristocracy, and sacred royalty itself, rested on farm and pasture. The man who wanted to rise in the world would rise automatically if he owned a proper homestead; security, social status, and political power would be his to enjoy and hand down to his children if he derived his living from his own acres. And these colonists, already hard to manage because land along the seaboard was so much easier to get than it ever could be in England or in Europe, now were looking west and perceiving that they had not yet scratched the surface. If they brimmed over the Allegheny crest and kept on toward the sunset, they would actually get the unlimited land that so far had been something out of dreams. There was enough here for millions upon millions of people, and the colonists were beginning to be well aware of it.

So the two problems, Indian country and seaboard colonies, came into contact and made one very great problem; so great, in the end, that it could not possibly be solved.

Once peace with France was made, the British had a substantial army in America with no foreign enemy to fight. It was necessary, for a time, to keep a good many soldiers in the west to tame dissident red men; then, after the government decreed that all the interior belonged to the Indians and that white settlers must not come west of the Alleghenies, it was necessary to maintain the army in order to enforce this edict. At about this time, the British discovered that it was proper, after all, to meet the Indian demand for gifts; and meanwhile, since it cost a good deal of money to keep this army on duty, it was essential to make the colonies contribute adequately to the army's support. This provoked unrest, increasing year by year, with hot protests against stamp acts and with chests of tea thrown into Boston harbor, so that more and more of the army had to be taken out of the Indian country and stationed along the Atlantic coast. In the high country, only a few of the most important places were held: Detroit and Michilimackinac, chiefly, as far as the Michigan country was concerned.

All of this trouble grew by what it fed upon, and presently the colonies were in full revolt, raising armies to fight the king's troops and at last ringing a great bell in Philadelphia to proclaim liberty. Like the Indians, the American colonists were a restless people, given to violent action. Also, they were discovering and being vastly irritated by the same thing that had irritated the Indians so greatly: the British really did not like them, considering them an inferior sort of people.

The Michigan country heard the American Revolution as a series of off-stage noises, which had no echoes whatever where the forest shadows were heavy. Most of the Indians knew about it only dimly, if at all, and cared not a whit. The French settlers were still numb from the shock of a lost war, and nobody bothered to tell them anything. Probably they would not have cared much, except for a dull feeling that it was good to see Les

Anglais in trouble. The English soldiers knew of course what was going on; but the war was a long way off, and it may have been hard for anyone on either peninsula to realize that the destiny of this land depended on what happened down by the Atlantic. Even that was problematical; it was quite conceivable that the colonies might wrench themselves free, but that the border would be drawn somewhere in western New York and Pennsylvania, leaving the northwest as it was. The foreground was full of Indians bringing furs or gathering, in blanketed ranks, to receive the king's bounty, with *habitants* tilling their acres and taking grain to the mill for grinding, with the occasional forty-ton sloop dropping down-river to try the Lake Erie road eastward; and with red coats and white cross-belts in formal lines across parade grounds to hear the thud of the sunset gun. It might well go on like this for a long time indeed.

Except for George Rogers Clark.

Clark was a husky Virginian, a civilized version of Major Rogers, gifted with a knack for getting along with Indians—probably because he actually liked them—and an even greater knack for inducing private soldiers to be as determined and enduring and contemptuous of danger as he himself was; a man who had a decisive influence on what was finally going to happen to the Michigan country and the whole northwest.

Clark was living evidence that the colonists were determined to expand westward. They had already overflowed into Kentucky, 25,000 of them; and in that dark and bloody land they were subject to unceasing forays by Indian warriors from north of the Ohio. They could not properly enjoy Kentucky until those Indians were suppressed, nor could their brother colonists move into the rich land north of the Ohio and make it their own, with every prospect of going on to the north and west wherever there seemed to be land worth occupying. Clark, who had raised a detachment of Kentucky riflemen in defense, in 1778 got orders from the governor of Virginia to cross the river and strike at the country that supported the Indian raiders. This seemed to be the Illinois country, where the British had taken over a chain of frontier posts from the French and where there were French settlements whose people raised crops, kept the peace with the Indians, and maintained a strip of country that was half European and half frontier-America. It made an ideal base to maintain Indian warriors willing to make war on colonists who were taking Indian land and rebelling against the English king, and Clark took his men down the Ohio in flatboats to the junction with the Tennessee, where they left the boats and started north, overland.

What they had to do was done quickly. They occupied the outposts of Kaskaskia, Prairie du Rocher, and Cahokia, neatly knocking the props out from under the war parties, and discovered that the French settlers were delighted to see them and happy to become citizens of the new republic far to the east. These people were so enthusiastic, indeed, that, when Clark sent a corporal's guard over to the Wabash, the people at Vincennes turned out to help them seize and occupy the British post there, Fort Sackville. The local Indians were willing to go along with this, and all was well: as a matter of fact, Clark had won the whole northwest for the United States, and the new nation the colonists had started had gained the ground that would enable it to grow and become great.

One man who realized this was Lieutenant Colonel Henry Hamilton, a tough British soldier who commanded the fort at Detroit. Hamilton struck back without delay, and toward the end of the year 1778, he took a force down through lower Michigan and across what is now northern Indiana and reoccupied Fort Sackville and Vincennes; he did this without much trouble, because the French settlers at Vincennes were not very warlike, and when the red-coats showed up, they subsided and accepted defeat. Hamilton might have gone on to the Mississippi, driving the Americans out of their conquest in the Illinois country: a good many of Clark's Kentuckians had drifted back home, and when winter came on, his force was slim. But it was a long way from Vincennes to Cahokia, and the winter turned nasty—lots of snow, but warm between storms, so that the snow melted, and half of Indiana was under water. Obviously, it would be impossible to make a 180-mile, cross-country march in all of this, so Hamilton snugged down at Fort Sackville and waited for spring.

The point about Clark is that he did not think that kind of march was impossible, so he went ahead and made it. His force had been whittled down to a low point, but he got recruits from among the French settlers in Illinois and set out, 180 men in buckskins splashing across an endless marsh in mid-winter, attempting an offensive that no sane man would have tried. Novelists and script-writers have exploited that offensive ever since, and no wonder. Colonel Hamilton had been right—it was impossible, Clark's men were up to their waists in ice-water through practically all of January, and most of the time their biggest problem was to find some place to spend the night where men could go to sleep without running the risk of drowning before morning. To this day, no one can figure out quite how they did it, but do it they did; and in mid-February, they reached Vincennes, soaking wet, two-thirds starved, and completely out of ammunition, facing an enemy who out-numbered them and who was snug and dry in a stout fort with shotted cannon to turn on starveling assailants. The townsfolk rallied round for Clark and dug up the ammunition and food Clark's men had to have, and he paraded them through the muddy streets of that skimpy frontier settlement, flags flying and drums beating, and then launched an assault on Fort Sackville—and carried the place, miraculously enough, Colonel Hamilton and his regulars surrendering meekly, and the northwest country was American. Clark considered going on to take Detroit, but sensibly concluded that he had tried his luck far enough and stayed where he was, which was intelligent of him because, without moving another step, he had made one of the most significant conquests in American history. When men sat down at Paris a few years later to write the peace treaty, it was obvious that the northwest country belonged to America.

Two interesting side effects followed on Clark's victory. The country west of the Mississippi was Spanish, and the Spaniards became encouraged and set out to try their hands at conquest: sent an expedition up the Illinois and Kankakee and captured the token stronghold of St. Joseph, on the Kankakee-St. Joseph portage. They held it only twenty-four hours and then went away, but they left a nice little story for the people of the town of

Niles, where old Fort St. Joseph used to be: it can boast, and properly does, that it is the only city in Michigan that has been under four flags—French, British, Spanish, and American.

The other side effect was farther north. When Clark captured Vincennes and Colonel Hamilton, what remained of British authority in the Michigan country took alarm and figured that Clark's incredible legion might well go four hundred miles to the north and seize Michilimackinac. And so, in 1780 and 1781, the British destroyed the old stronghold at the tip of the lower peninsula and moved across to Mackinac Island, where they built a new fort, one of the few forts in America—or anywhere else—that has actual charm, a beautiful contrivance of whitewashed stone going up a green hill to look out over blue water, with unbroken forests on the mainlands to north and south. In the fullness of time, it turned out that the fort had been poorly sited: the men who built it failed to notice that a nearby hill overlooked it, so that it could not be held if an attacker had the wit to climb that hill and haul a few cannon up there with him.

That was for the future, however. For the moment, one of the most beautiful places in America had been given a picture-book fort, as romantic as if war were a bloodless matter of handsome officers, dress-parade soldiers, and sunset guns echoing to infinity over the unending lakes. Father Dablon, at Marquette's old mission of St. Ignace, said that the fishing around Mackinac Island was so good that the Indians insisted this was the real homeland for whitefish and trout; however numerous they might be elsewhere, this was where they really came from. Warming to his subject—he apparently had the soul of a real fisherman—the good priest said that, in a very short time, a fisherman off Mackinac could get two dozen or more three-foot lake trout, and he added that these were by no means the largest: there was another kind, ready to be caught if a man persevered, that were "monstrous—for no other word expresses it." [3] Whatever its weakness and whatever its wealth in fish, Fort Mackinac was at

3. George R. Fuller, editor, *Historic Michigan*, 3 vols. (Lansing, Mich.: National Historical Association, Inc., 1924), I:96.

least surrounded by water too deep for Clark's amphibious warriors to wade. For the moment, it was secure.

Yet the security was only apparent. The long years that began when Champlain set out to see what kingdoms lay beyond Georgian Bay had been years of change, slow but inevitable, moving by lakes and rivers and dim forest trails to the last recesses of the wilderness; and now the process of change was about to be speeded up immeasurably and everything was going to be very different. When the Revolutionary War ended in 1783, the new nation was not only independent, but vastly enlarged, and it was going to have its heedless, uncalculated way with the land it had won. Its boundaries now were on the Mississippi, and north by Lake of the Woods and the bewildering mirages of Lake Superior, with Isle Royale as a haunting riddle lying beyond the horizon. In addition to the rich lands along the Ohio, the Wabash, and the Illinois, this new country included the two great peninsulas with their unending forests and the wealth hidden underground: a mysterious land, cool and aloof, waiting to be despoiled.

Having lost all this after so short a tenure, the British did not want to leave. They behaved now toward the verdict handed down at Yorktown much as the French had behaved toward the one delivered on the Plains of Abraham, acting as if nothing that happened in the east made any difference in the west. Garrisons that were supposed to withdraw to Montreal stayed where they were; most notably, Colonel Hamilton and his regulars hung on in Detroit, locking the door to all the Great Lakes country and cultivating the Indians with a warmth that Jeffrey Amherst would have considered most unsuitable. Indians to the south went on the warpath, and although the Americans sent expeditions against them, the expeditionary forces were badly disciplined and atrociously led and suffered humiliating defeats. The Indians obviously were getting both encouragement and military supplies from Detroit, and frontier America asserted that Colonel Hamilton was paying bounties for American scalps and referred to him as "the hair buyer." North and west of the scene of American defeats—roughly, the land below the Maumee River—things went on just as they had been before the war.

Then, at last, President George Washington decided to force a settlement. He put that stout Revolutionary veteran, Mad Anthony Wayne, in charge of the army and told him to go and break things up. With a methodical precision that belied his nickname, Wayne raised a proper force and spent a year drilling it, giving it both the equipment it needed and the demanding, sustaining discipline it needed even more—the steady professionalized discipline of the Continental Line. Then, in the summer of 1794, having the instrument he required, he marched north across western Ohio.

He found the Indians waiting for him, in a tangle of smashed trees that some tornado had piled up near the Falls of the Maumee: looked the situation over, hit hard, and broke the Indian force to fragments. Some of the fugitives swarmed up to a British army outpost in the vicinity and clamored to be let in, but the British officer there knew a losing hand when he had been dealt one, and he turned them away—at which point the Indians realized that the British had been using them but were not really going to help them when the crunch came. Within a short time, the leading men of the tribes that had been fighting came in to see Wayne and made peace meekly enough, opening all of the Ohio country to American settlers.

So this battle of Fallen Timbers was decisive. It ratified, on the frontier, the surrender terms signed at Paris more than a decade earlier. Great Britain saw the light, just as the Indians had seen it, and before long the north country was evacuated, and the Americans moved in. The flagpole at Detroit, which had worn the fleur-de-lis and then the banner of St. George, carried now the Stars and Stripes. And Niles, to be sure, got its fourth flag.

4

Governor Cass,
Governor Clinton,
and Mr. Astor

*M*EN said afterward that the great golden age of the woodland fur trade ended when the Americans took over Michigan. A good deal depends on the point of view, and on close examination the fur trade does not seem to have been exactly golden; it was as ugly and vicious as unbridled greed, and a good many of its practitioners were lawless thugs who defied the authorities, debased the Indians, and murdered each other with total absence of restraint. Yet the whole thing did have color and excitement, and, when all is said and done, it must be admitted that it was never dull. Lawless men have always captivated Americans, and what they did in Michigan was at least done against a backdrop of enchanting scenery. The Americans came in, not as reformers, but as accelerators. You can sum up the era by remarking that it began with Étienne Brulé, who went into the unknown and got a violent death for his pains, and closed with John Jacob Astor, who took over Brulé's heritage and became the richest man on the continent. The high country was under new management.

Congress created Michigan territory in 1805, and Astor organized his American Fur Company three years later. When he began, he found that, besides the far-off Hudson's Bay Company, there were two other big fur-trading concerns in being—the Northwest Company, which dealt with western tribes via the Grand Portage on Lake Superior, and the Mackinaw Company, which mostly covered Michigan. The trade was tightly controlled—as tightly as might be, that is, considering the fact that the independent woods runners were not easily controlled by anybody—but the British had put it on a different basis, and more and more the outlying posts were run by Englishmen, or Scots from Montreal, rather than by Frenchmen. This had come about very simply. The English had brought capitalism to the north woods.

Under the French, the fur country had been a huge game preserve, subject to a rapacity limited only by corruption, general inefficiency, and the inspired malfunctioning inevitable when profit-takers go to work with a *droit de seigneur* attitude. Both La Salle and Cadillac had offended against this system and had come to grief; the control was clumsy, exercised by stupid men, but it worked, and the old regime profited immensely. Then came the British, who liked the idea of a game preserve, but turned it over to the private monopolists, the gentlemen adventurers trading into Hudson's Bay, and the canny Scots from Montreal.

The great canoe brigades of the Northwest Company began to go to the top of the lakes, with little French Canadian crewmen back-packing prodigious loads over the portages, proud of their ability to endure man-killing labor and eat abominable food. (Unvarying ration, day after day: a kettle of peas cooked in lard, with a few ship's biscuit broken in.) Below Grand Portage, traders from the Mackinaw Company fanned out across the peninsulas, putting one-man posts far up rivers no one had ever heard of, pegging out the places where a man could go native and make a profit. Astor looked on and quietly began to buy into the Mackinaw Company; in half a dozen years, he had control, and it began to dawn on people that the lines now ran to New York, rather than to Montreal. And General William Hull, commanding U.S. forces at Detroit and also ruling the territory of Michigan, called a meeting of Potawatomis, Ottawas, Chippewas, and Wyandots and talked the tribesmen into giving up a fat slice of land—everything east of a north-south line drawn twenty miles inland from the western end of Lake Erie. The Indians got $10,000 in cash, soothing words, and certain annuities. The gate to the future had swung open.

It was not destined to go quite so smoothly as that. To begin with, Europe, in the early 1800s, was in the convulsion brought on by a world war, and America proved quite unable to stay out of it—particularly so because certain reckless Congressmen got the twin delusions that it would be nice to take over Canada and that now would be a good time to do it. In addition, a rangy Shawnee chieftain named Tecumseh took a leaf from Pontiac's book and concluded that, if the Indians of the Lakes stood together, they could, with British help, either exterminate the trespassing Americans or drive them out of the Indian heartland forever.

In the end, Tecumseh had no better luck than Pontiac had, but somehow he left a deeper impression on the American consciousness. The Americans feared him, fought him, and beat him, but they also respected him; and after it was all over, they even named towns and people after him: William Tecumseh Sherman, for instance. Legends clustered around him. It was said that, as a youth, he had fallen in love with a white girl in Ohio, that she promised to marry him if he would give up his wilderness heritage and adopt the white man's ways, and that, after spending a month in the forest, meditating, he went to her and told her he could not do it and said goodbye forever. Another legend (which does not quite harmonize with the first one) says that Tecumseh's mother took him, once each year throughout his youth, to the grave of his father and had him vow eternal enmity to the white man. Tecumseh had a brother, a one-eyed, hard-drinking visionary known as the Prophet, who seems to have been a second edition of the mystic who stirred Pontiac so deeply. Like his predecessor, the Prophet called on the red men to give up all of the white man's ways and live the Stone-Age purity of their forefathers. In 1811, the Prophet stirred up active hostilities during Tecumseh's absence, and William Henry Harrison led an army against him and shattered his forces at the village of Tippecanoe, in Indiana, thereby winning a nickname and setting the stage for a campaign jingle that would eventually carry him into the White House.

Tecumseh met with Harrison and argued bitterly about the way the whites were taking the red man's land. Harrison was reasonable enough, from his point of view: the whites negotiated with the proper Indian authorities, paid good money, got binding signatures on lawful treaties, and took nothing that they were not entitled to. Tecumseh—so angry that, at one point, he grabbed a tomahawk to settle the argument and was dissuaded by Harrison's bodyguard—held that all of this was a swindle. There were no Indian authorities, the Indian tribes that deeded land away were not competent to do anything of the kind, nobody could alienate land because it belonged to all the Indians, no matter what their tribal ties might be, and the treaties the Americans prized so highly meant less than the wind in the tree tops. After this meeting, Tecumseh went up to Lake Erie, crossed to Ontario, and went to confer with the British at Fort Malden, a post on the Detroit River from which the doings of the Americans might be observed. Tecumseh wanted to go to war, and he wanted to be sure he had the outside help that Pontiac only thought he had. Tecumseh picked a good time for it. The Canadian fur traders were getting irritated by Astor's encroachment and would be happy to see the Americans driven out of Michigan, and anyway America and England were drifting straight into war, and Tecumseh's ability to line up the Indian warriors would be a good asset, once the war began. Tecumseh and the British made a deal.

The war they anticipated was not long in coming. It opened with a series of American catastrophes; Tecumseh and his British friends had both energy and a clear understanding of the strategic possibilities of the situation, and they fought against men who seemed to have neither. Once in a while, Americans display a curious ineptitude when they go to war, and it was so here, in the year 1812. General Hull, at Detroit, had seen trouble coming, rightly enough, and had gone east to get reinforcements; he got them and was bringing them back, around the western end of Lake Erie, when he learned that the war had actually begun, and from that moment he could do nothing right. Reaching Detroit, he led troops across the river to destroy the British post at Malden, which he could easily have done; then he concluded that this idea was unsound, recrossed the river, learned that a party bringing supplies was being attacked by Tecumseh's Indians near the Raisin River, and sent a small force down to rescue this party. Tecumseh attacked the relieving force and made it return to Detroit, and a most competent British soldier, Major General Sir Isaac Brock, arrived from the east with reinforcements to take command at Malden.

Hull had more soldiers at his command than Brock had, but Brock knew how to use what strength he had, and Hull—well, Hull was a stout old smooth-bore, with a good record in the Revolutionary War, but he was in decay now and the fire was gone out of him, and when Brock led his men across the river and sent in a demand for surrender, Hull flabbergasted his officers by hanging out the white flag. On August 16, the Americans grounded their arms, and the Union Jack went up to the top of the flagpole at Detroit once more.

Nobody could hold the western country without holding Detroit, but it quickly developed that the British had taken the rest of it without much reference to Hull. The Potawatomis had swarmed down to menace Fort Dearborn, where Chicago is now, and Hull (before his own surrender) learned about it and advised the American commander to abandon the fort and take everybody east to Fort Wayne. The commander obeyed orders, notified the Indians that he was giving up the fort and that it would be theirs for the taking, and explained that he was going to make a nonviolent exit from their country. It seems that he tried their forbearance too far, because they were keyed up for a fight, and they were furious to learn that the departing Americans had destroyed the whiskey and the gunpowder with which the fort had been stocked; they ambushed him between the sandhills at the foot of Lake Michigan, and most of the Americans were massacred. On top of this, three hundred miles to the north, Fort Mackinac was taken.

The fort fell gently, without fighting and without bloodshed.

The American garrison consisted of fifty-odd men under Lieutenant Porter Hanks, and since it took a long time for news to reach the Straits from the Atlantic seaboard, these people, on July 17, did not yet know there was a war on; signs of impending trouble had been visible, but no one in the American government had thought to do what British General Brock did, who got speedy woods runners to take the news to the British post on St. Joseph Island, at the mouth of the St. Mary's River. The officer there quickly put together a mixed force—a few dozen redcoats, a larger number of Canadian militia, and a considerable contingent of Indians—embarked on one of the Northwest Company's schooners and several smaller craft, landed quietly at a cove on Mackinac Island out of sight of the fort, and moved to that forgotten hilltop that overlooked the fortifications, taking two brass cannon along. When morning came, Lieutenant Hanks was notified that, unless he immediately surrendered, these guns would start shooting down inside his fort, and on being assured that the Indians' tendency to slaughter prisoners would be restrained, he hauled down his flag. His captors lived up to their agreement, there was no massacre, and the last trace of American control over the Michigan country was gone.

So the War of 1812 was off to the worst possible start, with the high country lost—apparently beyond hope of recovery. A small expedition that tried to march up the old route from Ohio to Detroit the following year was waylaid along the River Raisin, where the Michigan city of Monroe now is, and, after a sharp fight, was compelled to surrender. The British gave the same pledge about keeping prisoners alive that had been given at Fort Mackinac, but this time it was observed only part way; some of the prisoners were taken intact up to Malden, but the wounded prisoners and certain others detained with them at the site of the battle were incontinently destroyed by Tecumseh's warriors, and the Americans of the west had a grim new war cry: "Remember the River Raisin!" It roused frontier fury properly enough, but although General Harrison (Old Tippecanoe himself, now and henceforward) was preparing to move up from Ohio, the odds were all against him. By this time, the Indians were convinced that the British were going to win the war, and they had no choice but to play along with the probable victors: especially with Tecumseh driving them on.

But the fate of the Michigan country was often determined by things that happened outside of Michigan. The country became British instead of French because of Wolfe's victory at Quebec, became American because Clark won at Vincennes, and passed under full American control because of Wayne's victory at the Fallen Timbers; and now it was all up to a United States naval officer named Oliver Hazard Perry. Displaying a prodigy of drive and industry not unlike that of Clark in the Vincennes campaign, Perry built and manned a serviceable fleet in a home-spun naval base on the Lake Erie shore, where the old French route from Fort Duquesne came down to the water, and toward the end of the summer, he sailed westward. Out in the Lake Erie islands, he found the British fleet, sailed in to engage it, and after a story-book fight in which he transferred his flag from a shot-riddled flagship to an undamaged craft, he sank or destroyed all of the British fleet—and the Americans had regained everything west.

With Lake Erie gone the British could not hold Detroit, and if they could not hold Detroit they could not hold any of the other places they had taken, and they knew it perfectly well. They evacuated Detroit; Old Tippecanoe pursued the retreating force to a place by the bank of the River Thames, in Ontario, fought and routed the Indian contingent, and killed that grim war chief Tecumseh. So the American flag went back up those flagpoles again, this time for keeps. It made no difference that an American attempt to re-take Mackinac failed; once Perry finished his day's work on Lake Erie, the island's number was up, and when the unhappy war at last dragged to its end, the north country was back in American hands, and no questions asked.

Apparently nothing had changed; but the United States government, having extricated itself from an apparently pointless war, did two things that suddenly accelerated the pace of Michigan's development beyond all calculation. It appointed Lewis Cass governor of Michigan Territory, and it decreed that hereafter only Americans could engage in the fur trade on American soil, which cleared the way for John Jacob Astor just when that embodiment of the acquisitive instinct was preparing to go into action. The two instruments that could most certainly bring about the change from deep wilderness to inhabited state had been placed where they could function effectively.

Cass was a young man who had been an officer in General Hull's army; he had made a good record there, before General Hull's surrender put the army out of action, and he was wholly dedicated to the idea that Michigan Territory must be developed, populated, and made prosperous. He undertook to get the Indians to surrender title to the land, saw to it that the land thus acquired was properly surveyed so that people could buy farms and building lots, and then made certain that the restless folk in the east and beyond the Atlantic who wanted to get homesteads in the virgin west knew about Michigan and directed their footsteps toward it. He was fantastically successful in all three ventures.

If Cass was devoted to the development of the territory's potentialities, Astor was devoted to the notion of making money. He had one basic idea about the way to exploit the natural resource that interested him, furs: take all there was, as quickly as possible, and then go on to something else. It was complained later that the lumber barons who destroyed Michigan's forests followed the simple rule of "cut and get out." That was precisely the rule Astor followed about the furbearing animals. Without intending to do anything of the kind, he cleared the way for Cass's program to induce the Indians to give up title to their land; through his agents, he destroyed the wild animals that were the mainstay of the Indians' way of life, and by the time Astor sold out—just before the boom collapsed—the Indians could do nothing but make the best deal they could and let the whites have the land that had ceased to be the fruitful wilderness on which Indian society was based.

Up to this point, Astor's company had to compete with the free British traders from Canada, not to mention the free Americans who operated out of Detroit. Now the British competition ceased, and Astor reorganized his company to take advantage of the situation. The entire region around the Great Lakes was set up as a separate department, with headquarters on Mackinac Island; a handsome building with a neat veranda, a magnet for tourists to this day, presided over then by two hard-hitting deputies, Ramsay Crooks and Robert Stuart. Working from a map and from detailed personal knowledge of the peninsulas, these men blocked out the various districts to be exploited and set up an organization very much like the kind that corporations a century later would set up to exploit markets of a different sort.

Each district got a manager, who was told where to put his headquarters and instructed to set up outposts (branch offices, a modern executive would say) where he thought they would be needed. District headquarters would consist of a log cabin and a log warehouse, situated at the mouth of some river that drained a spacious and fruitful hinterland, and the outposts would be placed as far up-river as a man in a canoe could readily go, with other outposts on the smaller rivers and swampy creeks that drained into the principal stream. Each outpost would be district headquarters in miniature, with a log cabin for the trader and if business were brisk enough, there would be another cabin to store furs.

To service all of this, there was an organization of fur brigades, each one consisting of half a dozen or more open boats known as "Montreal barges"—no longer the frail bark canoes of tradition, but regular planked batteaus, with crews to row them or, if necessary, to tramp along the beach and tow them, and with masts and sails to use when the wind was right. These craft would go down from Mackinac in October of each year, carrying goods to the several district headquarters—powder and shot, blankets, clothing, traps, cutlery, shoes, sometimes firearms—and at the inadequate river-mouth harbor maintained by district managers the goods would be transferred to the warehouses, from which place the district managers would put them in canoes for movement up-stream to the outlying posts. All of this movement, with luck, would be finished before the snows came, at which time each isolated trader would settle down to make a winter of it, trading with the Indians for furs. These outposts really were a long way from anywhere, and the wintering could be fairly rugged. In the spring, having disposed of his goods and obtained all the furs he could get, the trader would paddle down to the district headquarters, where in due time the fur brigades would pick up the winter's accumulations and take them back to Mackinac.

A good many rivers flow into Lake Michigan and Lake Huron, and Astor had a district manager at the mouth of just about every one. This took money and manpower—inside of two years, he had more than two hundred employees in the field, not to mention a good many semi-independent traders who handled his goods and sold him their furs—and the combination was more than most of the independent traders could resist. Some of them, to be sure, survived right down to the end, but most of them either gave up and left or made their own deals with Astor's people. Some of the independents he picked up in this way were fairly doughty people. Before the war of 1812, for instance, a trader named Joseph La Framboise, with his wife for company, went far up the Grand River to the rapids where the city of Grand Rapids was built years later and settled down for a winter's trading. In one way or another, he had aroused the Indians' enmity, and one day he was shot to death. Madame La Framboise was undaunted, and she stayed there, an independent trader, survived, and eventually was taken into the Astor organization.

When the United States took over the Lakes country, the government, yielding to a fit of high-mindedness, undertook to protect the Indian in spite of the fur trade, which was notoriously without conscience. To do this, it set up a number of factories, or regional trading centers, at which places the Indian could deal with Uncle Sam directly and so (at least, in theory) could buy his goods without being unmercifully fleeced. The idea was good, but the performance was bad: the bureaucrats put in charge of this operation were not salesmen and had no idea of the way in which buyers are to be cultivated, and the higher bureaucrats who stocked the warehouses were so smitten with a desire for economy that they laid in goods of most inferior quality. The Indians by this time had been buying things from the white man for many generations and were becoming sophisticated, and they knew shoddy merchandise when they saw it; they ceased to deal with the government's factories, and before long these were discontinued. The unfortunate part about it was that, from that time on, the Indians contemptuously referred to "American goods" as hopelessly third-rate.

One rule the government made had some odd results. It decreed that no trader could take whiskey into the wilderness and that anyone who did so would automatically forfeit his more solid wares to the tribes he was dealing with—and then it saw to it that the Indians were informed of this rule. In consequence, a trader plagued by an energetic rival had only to tip off the surrounding Indians that the rival had whiskey in his possession and then let nature take its course. All traders had whiskey, of course, because no trader with a proper eye on his cash balance would dream of going into the Indian country without it, and the Indians were delighted to help the Great White Father enforce his eccentric law by confiscating the stock in trade of the offending merchant.

What all of this means is that competition in the fur country was raised to an intensity never seen before. The American Fur Company moved into the Saginaw valley in 1828 to crush the independents there, and in a short time raised the take of muskrat skins there from 2,500 annually to 28,000, and got nearly 2,000 marten skins in place of 500. Up and down Michigan, the story was very much the same, with the result that long before it became a settled country the wilderness had lost most of its wild life. Astor was not the man to out-stay his time, and in 1834, he dissolved the American Fur Company, sold out, and turned his attention to matters in New York. Crooks bought out the old Great Lakes department and continued to operate from Mackinac under the old name, but the great days were over. Vast fortunes would continue to be made in Michigan—indeed, the surface had not yet been scratched—but they would no longer be made in furs.

What all of this meant was that the Indian was moving into the long sunset and that whatever happened to Michigan would happen without him. He would remain on the land as a legend and an unseen presence, leaving place names like Ontonagon and Kalamazoo and Tittabawassee; leaving also the haunted time of Indian summer, with corn-shocks rising like tepees in front of the flaming maples glowing through the autumn haze, and with the dark realities of neolithic savagery transmuted into romance for the small boys of the victorious palefaces. With all of this, subtly intertwined, went the French legacy, place names such as Au Sable and Charlevoix, Bois Blanc and Ile aux Galets and Presque Isle, and the memory of tough, bow-legged men who wore red sashes and sang Old-World songs while paddling leaky canoes to the end of the New World's cold blue lakes. The past was past, lost forever, Michilimackinac on a level with the ashes of Troy, Pontiac and Tecumseh gone to join Hector and Achilles; here was the future, coming in with axes and plows and immeasurable hopes to see what could be done with a fair country whose destiny thus far had been to supply the shops of Paris with felt hats and rich capes for the Versailles trade.

While the fur trade was still booming, Governor Lewis Cass moved to make certain that the people with axes and plows could legally buy the land that was waiting for them. The southeast corner of the lower peninsula was already out of Indian possession, properly surveyed and changed by that fact from wilderness to real estate. It was only a fragment of the whole, and Cass promptly acted to get the rest. A fur trader named Louis Campau had a trading post on a river bank where the city of Saginaw would some day be built, and in 1819 Cass went to see him and, with his help, persuaded the leading men of the Chippewa nation to surrender title to a vast stretch of territory enclosing Saginaw Bay, running up the Lake Huron shore to Thunder Bay, and including (although nobody quite realized it yet) some of the most magnificent stands of virgin pine in all North America. Two years later, again with the help of various fur traders, Cass talked the Potawatomis and Miamis into giving up the southwest quarter of the state; all the rest of the lower peninsula, together with a good half of the upper peninsula, became American soil in 1836—by which time, development had been advancing so solidly that full statehood was only one year away. By 1842, Indian title to all lands within the state's boundaries had been relinquished.

Arranging the treaties by which these huge parcels of land were acquired was not really very difficult. The Indians had got used to the white man, by now, and were more or less adjusted to the fact that he was there to stay; also, they got value received for the land they surrendered, receiving not only cash in hand and arrangements for annuities but also various continuing services—the help of blacksmiths to keep their guns in repair, schooling for their children, medical attention, some help (clumsy enough, but well-intentioned) in the matter of adapting to the new ways that American settlement would bring. It was remarked that the fur traders were quite helpful. From the beginning, unlike their French and British predecessors, they had known that civilization was going to come to the wilderness, and they had taken pains to be on friendly terms with the Indians and, by the standards of that time and place, to deal fairly with them; which is to say that although they did swindle them they kept it within bounds. As a result many of the Indians followed the traders' advice when it came to making treaties. One of Astor's most energetic agents, Rix Robinson, was largely responsible for arranging the cession of the last big block of land in the lower peninsula.

Then the land the settlers were going to want was processed so that they could get it, which means that the surveyors got busy. They began by carefully surveying and marking two lines—the meridian line, running north and south through the state on a true meridian of longitude, known as the "First Principal Meridian," and an east-west base line on a chosen parallel of latitude, which, as it turned out, ran along the northern border of Wayne County and continued on to Lake Michigan. Every piece of real property bought or sold in Michigan since then is described in terms of its relation to those two lines.

First, the surveyors laid out the country into townships six miles square, with each township thus containing thirty-six square miles. Measuring six miles along the base line to east or west of the Principal Meridian, the surveyor erected a monument and then ran another north-south meridian from it. From the principal meridian, in turn, at six-mile intervals, east-west lines were run, so that the whole state was laid out in a gigantic grid; and the long north-south strips running the length of the territory were known as ranges—No. 1 east, No. 5 west, and so on. The grid defined the townships, and each township in turn was measured off into thirty-six sections by parallel lines a mile apart: a section, accordingly, was one mile square and contained 640 acres, numbered from *1* to *36,* the top row reading from east to west, and next row coming west to east, and so on.

What all of this meant was that any forty-acre tract in the most remote part of the territory could be precisely located by a description such as "The southeast quarter of the northwest quarter of Section 17 in Township 8 north Range three east of the Principal Meridian." A man whose land was recorded so had an incontestable title, with no ambiguities. While all this surveying was going forward, a new land law passed in 1820 made it possible for a man who could pay cash to buy eighty acres of land at $1.25 an acre; which meant that, for as little as $100, he could become the owner of an eighty-acre farm. If the soil was halfway good and he was strong and industrious, he was fixed for life. Since time began, no one had ever seen the likes of this.

It remained to bring the prospective owners into contact with the empty land, and here there were problems; Michigan just then was extremely hard to reach, and hardly anybody supposed that the soil was worth owning even when you got there. This was partly the fault of Divine Providence, which had put extensive swamps right where the incoming settlers would want to drive their wagons, and partly the fault of a man named Edward Tiffin, surveyor-general of the United States.

Immediately after the close of the war of 1812, Tiffin sent in men at the request of Governor Cass to survey the land taken over from the Indians—at that moment, a good-sized stretch of land running from the Ohio line halfway up the Thumb. Tiffin's men toiled and struggled, did their job, and reported in disgust that the whole territory was nothing but a swamp; Tiffin in turn reported that the country was a land of swamps, lakes, and sandhills, and cited an earlier report to Thomas Jefferson by James Monroe asserting that the region "will never contain a sufficient number of inhabitants to entitle them to membership in the confederacy."[1] It was pointed out that Joseph Meigs, superintendent of the General Land Office, considered that hardly one acre in a thousand was fit for cultivation. In 1822, the War Department built a fort where Saginaw is now, and in less than a year the major commanding, noting that the entire garrison, including himself, was down with malaria except for one enlisted man, declared bitterly that only "Indians, muskrats and bullfrogs"[2] could ever live on the Saginaw River. Apparently the War Department believed him, because the new post was abandoned.

So Michigan got a very bad press, and there was some reason for it. To reach this area, in those days, people from the east usually crossed Pennsylvania overland, drifted down the Ohio, and then cut north overland, striking up for the mouth of the Maumee, where Toledo is now. This place, unfortunately, was virtually surrounded by a vast bog known as the Black Swamp, which was no fit place for an immigrant wagon. Worse yet, the country around Detroit, for twenty miles west and south, was an old lake bottom, subject to flooding in wet weather, the soil a sticky clay set off with many marshes and ponds that could be crossed only with great difficulty. Eventually, of course, the land could be drained, as could the Black Swamp around Toledo, but that had not yet been done. As late as 1836, when a road was built from Detroit to Pontiac, the first twelve miles had to be corduroyed.

This meant that, as far as a prospective land-buyer was concerned, Michigan was hard to reach; worse yet, it would be quite impossible to ship farm produce out of it at a profit, because transporting bulk freight by wagon over hundreds of miles was ruinously expensive. In consequence, takers for Michigan real estate were not very numerous. In 1818, someone built a steamboat, the famous *Walk-in-the-Water,* which ran from Buffalo to Detroit, and this was fine in a way, but for the

1. John Anthony Caruso, *The Great Lakes Frontier* (Indianapolis: Bobbs-Merrill Co., Inc., 1961), p. 351.

2. Caruso, *Great Lakes Frontier,* p. 361.

fact that Buffalo itself was not much of a market and was a long, long way from the eastern seaboard.

But all through those early days, Michigan's destiny was often determined by things that happened a long way off, and so it was now. In 1825, the Erie Canal was opened, Buffalo to the Hudson, and suddenly Detroit was easily accessible to the populous east and eastern markets were accessible to Michigan farmers. A strong tide began to flow. It developed that the east contained many people who had heard Governor Cass's siren song and wanted to go to Michigan to live, and they came up the new canal and clamored for transportation to Detroit. There were so many of them that there was sharp competition between Buffalo and the Niagara River port of Black Rock to see which place would be the hub of the new trade route to the west. Little *Walk-in-the-Water* could not begin to carry everybody, and in no time at all there were six steamboats shuttling the length of Lake Erie, with more to come.

Not all of these people were headed for Michigan, of course. Ohio had already become a state and needed an eastern outlet for its farm produce, and the boats from Buffalo cruised along the south shore of Lake Erie and found business especially good at Cleveland, where the Ohioans were busy digging a canal of their own to provide water transportation between the lake and the Ohio River. But the Michigan trade was brisk, and growing, and in 1836, a new steamboat line was organized to run between the Erie Canal and the Detroit River. As might be supposed, Lewis Cass was one of the stockholders.

In the beginning, Michigan had nothing to ship east except furs, and in 1826, furs worth $200,000 went down the lake to Buffalo and Black Rock. But in less than ten years, wheat was beginning to move; and by 1841, Detroit shipped 180,000 bushels of flour, 12,000 barrels of whiskey, and—sign of great things soon to come—sawed lumber worth $75,000. The Erie Canal was not ten years old before the authorities of New York State realized that it would have to be enlarged. In 1829, the Canadians opened the Welland Canal between Lake Ontario and Lake Erie, and freight from Detroit and Cleveland could now move to Montreal without trans-shipment—a powerful stimulus to the thinking of the New York merchants.

In any case, what had been the remote wilderness of Michigan had in effect been moved hundreds of miles closer to civilization, and the wilderness was being dismantled with all due speed. To the list of names of men who had never been there whose acts had profoundly affected Michigan's destiny, from James Wolfe down to Oliver Hazard Perry, it was now necessary to add one more: De Witt Clinton, who put through the Erie Canal.

5

Statehood

$\mathcal{S}$O far, events had been leisurely. Two centuries after Champlain, the peninsulas were about as they had been when he arranged to send a bright young man up to the high country. There were half a dozen settlements now, most of them still wearing the bark and shade of the forest, and there was a scattering of traders' cabins and woods runners' wigwams dotted about at long intervals; and in a land where nothing had happened since the glaciers melted, these of course represented change. But the change had come one step at a time, to be measured in decades and generations. In two centuries, nothing in particular had happened.

Now there was a big speed-up, with a century of change compressed into a few years. Between LaMothe Cadillac and Henry Ford, there are just two hundred years, and the Detroit of Lewis Cass was at the halfway point—except that measuring it so makes no sense at all. Cadillac would have recognized Cass's Detroit as a piece of the world he knew; there was no way on earth by which he could have recognized Ford's Detroit, because it was part of an entirely different world inhabited by men whose eyes were adjusted to things the eighteenth century could not see. The biggest and fastest change in history grew out of certain intangibles and a few small physical problems, such as the need of Michigan's early settlers to find quicker ways to move from here to there.

The biggest intangible of all was the fact that necessitous men suddenly found themselves facing an era of dazzling, incomprehensible abundance. The age-old restraints that in all generations compelled men to struggle against long odds, and also against each other, to get not-quite-enough of the things they had to have to stay alive, seemed to have disappeared forever. Men who broke into this new country fairly babbled when they wrote to people back east and tried to tell what they had found: land enough and to spare, at a fraction of the price men paid elsewhere, so productive that it was not to be described soberly. A farm field was "a carpet of wild strawberries" all the way. Michigan was "the El Dorado of agricultural emigrants from both sides of the Atlantic," a land so rich that, in trying to appraise its yield, "the mind becomes bewildered, and mistrusts its own considerations." A man who laid out a farm on the Huron River in 1825 said this country was unlike any he had ever seen before, and better: "The interior of Michigan is delightful—a mixture of prairies, oak openings and woodland, abounding in clear streams, fine lakes and cold springs . . . a rolling country well adapted to good roads." [1]

Men hearing about a magic land such as that wanted above all other things a way to get into it, and the boats on the Erie Canal were crowded. Rates were fantastically low, all things considered: one cent a mile per passenger, two cents if the boat company provided food, five cents for an "express" boat that traveled day and night. The boats were long, oblong blocks, inexpressibly clumsy and sluggish by modern standards, representing, in the late 1820s, an unheard-of speed: one of the express packets could go a hundred miles in twenty-four hours, as much as an emigrant wagon could do in a week and, on the whole, much more comfortable.

The comfort of course was comparative. The main cabin was narrow, low-ceilinged, fuggy as the black hole of Calcutta, both sides lined with bunks, tables in the center for meals, bar and

1. Ronald Shaw, "Michigan Influences upon the Formative Years of the Erie Canal," in *Michigan History,* XXXVII, no. 1:7, 10.

galley at the rear, tiny cabin for women passengers forward, means of ventilation grossly inadequate and shut off entirely in rainy weather. To stay alive most passengers remained on deck as much as they could, although someone had to stay alert and give the warning cry, "Low bridge!" so that everyone could lie flat when the boat passed under a highway bridge, the overhead clearance being almost nonexistent. All in all, it was no pleasure excursion, although in the main the travelers seem to have kept up good spirits; they were moving more rapidly and more cheaply than they had ever expected to do, and the fact that the freight rate (on farm produce or on household goods) had abruptly dropped from the freight wagoner's thirty-two dollars a ton to a flat dollar tended to help people to overlook incidental hardships. Besides, this was not an era when people really expected to be very comfortable, anywhere.

At Buffalo, the folk who wanted to go to Michigan changed from canal packet to deep-draft Lake Erie steamer—or, in some instances, to schooners or sloops, because most of the common carriers at this time moved under canvas—and the accommodations were a little less straitened than those on the canal, although Lake Erie was often stormy, the boats were all rather small, and a battened-down cabin containing two dozen mortals who had been seasick for twenty-four hours or more can hardly have been attractive. With whatever difficulties, the steamer or windjammer finally got to the western end of Lake Erie, and now the really trying part of the trip began.

Most of the travelers disembarked at Detroit, although some were put ashore at Monroe, a settlement that had sprung up around the mouth of the River Raisin, and others went to Port Lawrence, near the mouth of the Maumee, a place that presently changed its name to Toledo. No matter which port he used, the emigrant now found himself obliged to travel over roads that were just a hand's breadth short of being altogether impassable.

From Detroit, a trace called the Old Sauk Trail led down across the southern part of the peninsula, following an old Indian route. This road was particularly atrocious in its first portion. Harriet Martineau, in 1836, reported bitterly that "Juggernaut's car would have been 'broke to bits' on such a road," [2] and a Detroit newspaper in the same year said that the road was lined with so many wrecked wagons that it looked like the route followed by a defeated army flying in headlong retreat. From the Monroe area, what was known as the La Plaisance Bay trail came up northwesterly to intersect this road; and a little farther along, there was a similar road slanting up from the Maumee country in Ohio. Governor Cass saw to it that a territorial road was driven west north of the Old Sauk Trail, following the Kalamazoo River valley for a distance and coming out (some years later) at the mouth of the St. Joseph River and the twin ports of St. Joseph and Benton Harbor, where those bound for Illinois or Wisconsin could take steamers to Chicago. Stagecoach lines had been established on these roads, and at intervals of twenty miles or so, there would be an inn to provide food and lodging and a change of horses. Around these inns, little towns began to develop.

No matter which route an immigrant took, the first twenty miles or so carried him across an old lake bottom, a heavy clay soil just above water in dry weather and partly or wholly under water when the weather was bad. When it rained, which sometimes it did for days at a time, a loaded wagon was likely to sink down until the wagon bed rested flat on the tenacious mud, the wheels buried to the axles. Then there was nothing for it but to go into the woods and cut timbers that could be used to pry the wagons loose, and at times different parties would club together and use double or triple teams to haul their wagons out, painfully, one at a time. Now and then, of course, the wagon just had to be abandoned, which accounts for the wreckage the Detroit newspaper man had noticed. Learned debates were held, at night, when men had supper and sat around fires to get dry; was it better to stick to the roadway, or to haul out and try to go along the unimproved land beside it? When the whole countryside was under water, it probably did not make much difference, and the actual roadway itself was so close to being unimproved that a turn-out could easily be advisable. One trou-

2. Fuller, *Historic Michigan*, I:244.

ble was that so many drivers turned out that the land beside the road was apt to be rutted more deeply than the road itself. The going was bad, whatever one did.

By no means all of the newcomers moved by stagecoach. A great many came in by wagon, possibly a majority of all immigrants: in 1836, a man given to counting things reported that one wagon left Detroit for the interior every five minutes, dawn to dusk, from early spring to late autumn. Many of the wagon parties came by boat from Buffalo, wagon beds flat on deck, wheels lashed in the rigging, immigrants as likely as not sleeping in the immobilized wagons. At Detroit, the wagons would be put ashore and fitted together again, and the family would start west, setting its course by whatever maps and directions might be available.

Other wagons came up from Ohio or Indiana, overland. Many of the frontiersmen were restless, and men who had settled in the Ohio country often sold out, loaded their goods and families in wagons, and set out for the Michigan country, driving their livestock ahead of them. Others were Southerners who came up across the Ohio River and followed some migratory instinct to the Michigan country. Frequently, several families would club together to make a long caravan much like the bigger ones that headed for Oregon and California a few years later. People who moved this way were usually people of some means, and in a combined operation, they had enough manpower to get out of the mud-holes without calling for help. In mid-summer, when everything was dry, nobody got stuck in the mud, but the roads were deep in dust that concealed chuckholes that could break an axle and made walking more pleasant than riding. It was noticed that, in summer, there was a great plague of mosquitoes; a few years later, it was also noticed that malarial chills and fever afflicted almost all of the settlers, until the land got properly cleared and the swamps were drained.

However difficult traveling conditions were, there is universal testimony that the newcomers found the trip worth the trouble. The lower part of Michigan, which was all of Michigan these people saw in those first decades of the nineteenth century, was by no means the dark, pine-forest country of tradition. Here there were groves of hardwoods, and stretches of actual prairie, and the oak openings that lay like semiformal breaks on the easy slopes. The soil was rich, the woods growth was so open that a man could see something of the country when he looked around him, and the wilderness obviously would be easily tamed. (Comparatively easily, at any rate: the settlers quickly learned that it took a great deal of hard work to carve out and bring to cultivation a farm in this new country.) An English settler wrote home that the country looked like "a gentleman's park." [3] He had money enough to buy eighty acres of land, and he wrote jubilantly to his relatives beyond the Atlantic:

> I must give you my opinion of this country and England and draw some comparison between them. I have left England and its gloomy climes for one of brilliant sunshine and inspiring purity. I have left the country cowring with doubt and danger where the rich man trembles and the poor man frowns, where all repine at the present and dread the future. I have left this country and am in a country where all is life and animation, where I hear on every side the sound of exultation, where everyone speaks of the past with triumph, the present with delight, the future with growing confidence and anticipation. Is not this a community in which one may rejoice to live? Is not this a land in which one may be proud to be received as a citizen? Is not this a land in which one may be happy to fix his destiny and ambition? I answer for one. Am I asked how long I mean to remain here I answer as long as I live. [4]

This man had taken a farm in one of the best parts of what would soon be famous as the middle-western farm belt, and later letters show that he developed his acres, bought more, and prospered; yet it is clear that what was touching him off when he wrote this jubilant letter was not so much the wealth of the soil as something in the air he breathed. He was saying what all of these immigrants felt, what sustained them on that impossible trip and helped them bear up under the difficulties of building new homes in a land plagued by crippling chills and fever and

---

3. John Fisher, "Letters from Michigan," in *Michigan History,* XLV, no. 3:221.
4. Fisher, *Michigan History,* XLV, no. 3:224–225.

remote from the amenities of civilized society: the great feeling
that, out here, they had escaped from the restricting past and
had reached a land where personal freedom was a living reality.
The dream that led men and women across the ocean had
always dangled a little way in front of them, never quite
reachable, leading them on but not letting them overtake it.
Now, suddenly, incredibly, they had it. They meant to remain
here as long as they lived.

Early in the nineteenth century, an Ottawa Indian who would
become known as Chief Andrew Blackbird was born, up in the
L'Arbre Croche region. He took up the white man's way, went
to the university for a white man's education, got it, and returned to the region of his boyhood to become postmaster at
Harbor Springs. A few years later he wrote a book, and at one
place he tried to say what life had been like when he was
young. Life then, he said simply, was idyllic: "Such an abundance of wild strawberries, raspberries and blackberries that
they fairly perfumed the air of the whole coast . . . I never
knew my people to want for anything to eat or to wear . . . I
thought (and yet I may be mistaken) that my people were very
happy in those days." [5]

At about the time Chief Blackbird wrote his book, a woman
whose parents had come into lower Michigan with the first wave
of settlers looked back on her girlhood on a farm not far from
Jackson and saw pretty much what the Ottawa had seen: peace,
plenty, and happiness. Her mother's kitchen, she recalled, was
bare and probably primitive, but

> I can certify to the quality of the cooking, for the very walls of the
> kitchen were permeated with odors of roast meat, salt-rising bread,
> spice cake, gingerbread—a whole roster of fragrant memories, tan-
> talizing to the nose and stimulating to the palate. . . . In such a
> room as this, inconvenient, poorly equipped for the work to be done
> in it, arranged with absolutely no thought to saving steps or labor,
> freezing cold in winter until the morning fire was lighted, hot in
> summer until the stove was allowed to cool off in later afternoon,

5. May and Brinks, *A Michigan Reader,* p. 34.

but homely in comfort, with cheerful, even charming atmos-
phere—here was cooked the food which, as I think about it, still
makes my mouth water.[6]

All of these people were saying much the same thing: the
recently arrived Englishman, the educated Indian, and the pioneer's daughter. Life was *good* then, there was plenty, and people enjoyed it, they were suspended half-way between the trials
of yesterday and the hideous problems of tomorrow, and just to
be alive and here was enough for anybody. There is a folk
memory of such things, and a desire to regain them. . . .

As the people came in, the little towns were born: Ann
Arbor, Adrian, Tecumseh, Niles, Ypsilanti, and Jackson and
Kalamazoo, Battle Creek and Grand Rapids, Coldwater and
Grand Haven—a long list, little no-places at first, some destined
for a large future, some not. A man from the village of Tecumseh, visiting in Detroit, was asked where he came from and
named the place. "Tecumseh? Where's that?" he was asked.
With the rueful patience of a man who realizes that his home
town is unknown to fame and likely to remain so, he replied
that Tecumseh was "thirty miles beyond Monroe and forty
miles beyond God's blessing." [7] In the year before the Erie
Canal was opened, fewer than 62,000 acres of Michigan soil
had been sold, all of it in the Detroit area. By 1826, nearly one
and one-half million acres had been sold in and around Detroit
alone, with corresponding increases elsewhere in the state. Cass
had pushed the survey, so that ten million acres had been
marked out, and land offices were opened at Monroe, White
Pigeon, and Kalamazoo. They were most active, and the saying
"Doing a land-office business" passed into usage as a way to
say that business was booming. There was a lonely spot where
the trail from Detroit to the Saginaw country crossed the Flint
River, at a little rapids; a trader named Jacob Smith put a cabin
there in 1819 and helped Cass make his deal with the Indians;

6. Della Lutes, *The Country Kitchen* (Boston: Little, Brown and Company, 1938),
pp. 22–23.
7. Clara Waldron, *One Hundred Years a Country Town: The Village of Tecumseh,
1824–1924* (Jackson, Mich.: Thomas A. Riordan, 1968), p. 33.

MICHIGAN
A photographer's essay by Joe Clark, HBSS

Photos in Sequence

and in 1830, one John Todd built a tavern and began to operate a ferry. Six years later, the government had a land office there, and observant men began to realize that there was a fine stand of pine timber a little way upstream and that the swift flow of water here would power a sawmill. There was also a road to market, because, below the rapids, the river wound its way into other streams and eventually into Saginaw Bay, so that the sawed lumber could be floated out inexpensively. The first thing anyone knew, there was a town named Flint, due to grow larger.

It was not the timber that pulled the early settlers, however. The forest was looked upon as an encumbrance, rather than an asset. When a new town was founded, one of the first buildings to be put up (provided water power was available, which was not always the case) was a sawmill, but that was simply so that the people who built houses there could have the logs they removed from their acres turned into the planks and joists and beams they needed. The lumber was of no cash value. Where all transportation had to go by wagon over roads that at best were just barely passable, no one was going to try to send lumber off to market. Where there was no sawmill—if the stream on which the town was situated lacked fall enough to turn a mill wheel—men just built log cabins and waited for better times.

The forest meant very hard work for the settler: so much that nowadays one is apt to wonder how on earth any of them accomplished it. The first thing, of course, once some sort of shelter was provided, was to clear enough ground to get in a crop, and a lone man with no help but a couple of teen-age sons and no power resources except for a team of oxen faced serious problems. If his land contained a bit of prairie or one of the fabled oak openings, he could make a start at once, but if it did not, he had to find some way to raise wheat and corn and potatoes in the middle of the woods. He would girdle as many trees as possible, stripping off the bark in a broad band completely encircling the trunk. The girdled trees would quickly die and shed their leaves; and then, with luck, enough sunlight would come in to make it possible to raise a crop of sorts—enough, at least to get the family through the coming winter. If the man had brought livestock, pigs could forage for themselves in the woods, and much of the time cows could do the same although if they ate wild onions, or leeks, their milk became virtually undrinkable. If the settler did have cows and oxen or horses, he had to build some sort of log barn for them to occupy in cold weather.

It was still necessary to fell the dead trees, and after the crop was in, he would get at it, with his axe. Branches from the down timber could be cut up into firewood, but in most cases there was nothing at all to do with the trunks; so great bonfires were built, and incalculable amounts of perfectly good wood went up in smoke. If a little potash could be shipped out, so much the better, but the big idea was to clear the land. This was farming country, and first-rate farming country at that, and that was all anyone cared about. It has been estimated that the state of Michigan actually burned up more timber than the enormous quantity it eventually sent to market as lumber, and if the hardwood that later was consumed to make charcoal for backwoods iron furnaces is included, the estimate is probably correct.

It might be added that the farmer's family made its own soap, and, if it had cows, made its own butter, and if it had brought along any sheep (as thousands of settlers did), it also made its own clothing. One of the few bits of household equipment the immigrant wagons almost always carried was a spinning wheel. Most of the family's furniture was made at home, at least in the early days. The farmer might be an indifferent cabinet maker, but people who have to move all of their worldly goods in an ordinary wagon over a 500-mile pull cannot carry very many chairs, tables, and bedsteads.

In one way or another, the job got done, and the southern tiers of Michigan counties were solidly established. Their big problem now began to be, in a more intense form, the same one that had beset them when they were trying to get in: transportation. There were fields to raise surplus crops of wheat and corn, and grist mills to reduce the grain to flour or meal, and animals to provide salt beef and salt pork for export, but to send these out by wagon was ruinously expensive. (Item: one staple the farmer then had to have, if he were to preserve his beef and pork, was salt, which was fearfully costly; a barrel of salt delivered in the new town of Adrian cost fifteen dollars, and exactly half of this sum was the cost of bringing it in by freighter's wagon from Toledo, which was just thirty miles away.) In the first flush of enthusiasm, lighted by the success of the Erie Canal, Michigan thought of building canals of her own, and fine plans were laid for a ditch that would run completely across the base of the peninsula, from Lake Erie to Lake Michigan. Nothing ever came of them.

For a time, it looked as if there might be an Indian war to make the settlers' situation impossible. Over beyond Lake Michigan, the great chief Black Hawk banded the Sauk and Fox people together, and in 1832 he made a last, despairing effort to drive the white man away so that Indian life could go on in the old way. There were people in Michigan who feared the worst. They had some reason to do so, for most of the area now being settled was Potawatomi country, and the Potawatomis were not placid Indians; they had performed the massacres at Fort Dearborn and on the River Raisin, they had provided Tecumseh with a good deal of his manpower, and Black Hawk was making overtures to them. The Old Sauk Trail, which was still the principal route between Detroit and the Illinois country, was the route followed by Illinois tribesmen who once a year tramped to the Detroit River and crossed over to Malden to collect gifts from the British, who seem to have had a lingering notion that there might again be war with the up-start Americans. Now it was rumored that Black Hawk and his warriors would come up this trail with evil intent, picking up Potawatomi braves as they advanced, and Tecumseh's work would be started all over again with a firebrand and hatchet for settlers' cabins all the way west.

Long afterward, the son of a fur trader who had been born at L'Arbre Croche and grew up more Indian than white man recalled that, at the end of 1831, he was settling down for the winter in a little Indian village at the northeast corner of Crystal Lake, which was about as far into Indian country as a man could get. To this village came a couple of war chiefs from Black Hawk, and a council of the tribe's head men was called to hear them. After the proper formalities, the men from the south got up to have their say: Black Hawk was going to make war on the white men and he wanted the Michigan Indians to drive the white intruders out of their country and kill all who might resist. The visitors enlarged on the bad deeds of the whites, with much impassioned oratory. (Fortunately for him, the trader was accepted by the Indians as an Indian himself, and was able to sit through all of this unharmed.) When the oratory ended, the head man of the Crystal Lake village arose to reply. The white man, he said, had been kind to his people, and nobody had anything against him. Further, the whites were far too strong to be beaten, and to go to war now would mean the burning of Indian villages and the slaughter of Indian women and children. The other local dignitaries spoke in the same vein, and at last Black Hawk's men went away and nobody ever heard anything more about it. Black Hawk had his war, but it was accompanied by no troubles in Michigan.

Lewis Cass had done his work well. The Indians both respected him and liked him, calling him "Big Belly" in friendly tribute to his ample girth, and the final flare-up of Indian warfare in the Middle West did not touch the territory he was responsible for. He had talked the Michigan Indians into surrendering most of their homeland to the whites, and obviously they did not feel that they had been swindled. They trusted him, after the bargain as well as before it; in the years just ahead, they would give up the rest of their country at his behest, and if they finally became melancholy, they did not become bitter. As a matter of fact, even the Potawatomis had become adjusted, and settlers along the Kalamazoo found them quite friendly, in a taciturn-red-man sort of way. This unhappily did the Potawatomis no good, and a few years later, the federal government moved them bodily to the far side of the Mississippi: the federal government at the time was principally Andrew Jackson, who had fixed ideas about moving Indians out of land the white man wanted.

In 1831, Lewis Cass ceased to be governor of Michigan Territory, Jackson having called him to Washington and made him Secretary of War. This did not end Cass's association with

Michigan affairs. For one thing, he remained a legal resident, with a fine home in Detroit; for another, Indian affairs at that time were under the general supervision of the Secretary of War, and the Indian agent in upper Michigan was Henry Schoolcraft, who had gone with Cass when Cass made an extensive canoe trip from Detroit to the far-off headwaters of the Mississippi in 1820. When Schoolcraft dealt with the Indians— as he did, most extensively, during the next few years—he did so as agent of Secretary Cass. In addition, the Secretary of War had a good deal to say about the need for military roads in an undeveloped territory such as Michigan, and the road that was put through from Detroit to the shore of Lake Michigan at the mouth of the St. Joseph was put there largely on Cass's insistence.

Untouched by the Black Hawk war, Michigan nevertheless had somber reason for remembering the event. In 1832, the federal government sent regular troops out to Fort Dearborn to make certain that this new Indian war did not get out of hand, and four steamboats full of soldiers with Winfield Scott in command cleared from Buffalo and set out on the long round-the-horn trip to the foot of Lake Michigan. They stopped at Detroit, and suddenly it developed that the soldiers were coming down with Asiatic cholera. The contingent included a number of new recruits and these gave way to panic, jumping ship and running off aimlessly into lower Michigan, fleeing from the mysterious contagion but actually carrying it with them. There was cholera in Michigan now, and as news of it spread there was an abrupt halt in the tide of new settlers. Scott stopped the desertions, and as soon as possible continued on the water route to Chicago; he knew nothing about the way to treat cholera (sharing the ignorance held by the medical profession generally), but he did understand military discipline, and he kept his men in hand for the balance of the trip. A horrifying number of men died, but at least the panic was checked, although it is recorded that a comparatively small number of the troops sent west ever saw service against Black Hawk's warriors. The cholera scare died down finally, but it had killed many settlers and Michigan was a long time forgetting it.

Once the terrors raised by Black Hawk and the cholera died down, the flow of emigrants from the east was resumed, and the Michigan settlers realized anew that their real enemy was not the wilderness and its lurking perils, but simple distance. In 1832, the government had ordered a military road put through from Monroe on Lake Erie to cut into the Detroit-Chicago road, but this obviously was not the real answer. Now a brand new clamor was heard: *build some railroads.*

Railroads were a new thing, little understood, but most promising. There was one in New Jersey and another in South Carolina; a few more lines were under development in the east, and Ohio was talking about putting a line through from Sandusky to the Ohio River, to supplement the north-south canals that were being built. Almost all of the new lines built or projected were stub lines, designed either to connect two waterways or to give a hinterland access to a seaport; water transportation was the big thing, but apparently these new railroads would make admirable supplementary lines, or feeders, and as such they looked like the answer to Michigan's prayer. In the territorial capital, Detroit, charters for a large number of railroads were drawn up and issued.

To get a charter and draw interesting lines on a map was simple enough, but to raise money, survey a right of way, and then actually build a line was something very different. The first group to go all the way with the process was composed chiefly of men from the thriving little city of Adrian, who got a charter to construct something called the Erie and Kalamazoo Railroad, raised some money, and then went to work to make the railroad a reality. Their basic plan was conventional enough: connect Lake Erie at the mouth of the Maumee—Port Lawrence, or Toledo—with navigable water on the Kalamazoo River that flowed west to Lake Michigan. ("Navigable" by the standards of that time and place, when water for canoes and batteaux was good enough, with sufficient depth for a small shallow-draft steamboat regarded as a good bonus.) It would of course take time to put the line as far as the river, but the thirty miles between Toledo and Adrian could be built right away, and that would be a fine thing for Adrian and indeed for all settlers bound for the interior, because it would provide good transportation across the bad swamps.

Nobody on earth really knew much about building a railroad, in those days, and it was trial and error all the way. The Erie and Kalamazoo people followed what looked like good practice: once the right of way was cleared and made approximately level (and the word *approximately* could be construed quite loosely), squared beams were laid parallel on cross-ties, and a car on flanged wheels could be drawn along this by horses. It would develop before long that strips of flat iron ought to be laid along the inner edges of the long beams, and a little later still it would become obvious that these should be replaced by regular iron rails, and the need to put the horses out to grass and bring in regular steam engines would also be made clear by events, but for the moment even the primitive affair of horse-drawn cars rolling along wooden rails was an enormous advance over any other form of transportation anywhere in Michigan, and work on the new railroad went forward gaily.

Before the project was finished, it ran into unexpected problems. It was to connect Adrian and Toledo, and now it developed that nobody knew whether Toledo was in Ohio or Michigan; furthermore, nobody quite knew who was running Michigan, and for a time it seemed possible that the state of Ohio and the territory of Michigan would come to blows, staging a miniature civil war far ahead of time. It was all most confusing, and the fact that it had rowdy slapstick-comedy overtones did not make the problem less real.

By an act of Congress dating from the earliest days of independence, the northern boundary of Ohio west of Lake Erie was an east-west line drawn from the southern tip of Lake Michigan. Nobody then knew just where that tip might be, and nobody cared very much, but eventually it was seen that the point was farther south than had been supposed; so, when Ohio came into the Union in 1803, she brought along a constitution saying that the boundary line must be tilted so that the mouth of the Maumee River would lie in Ohio. This did not seem especially important, at the time, but Maumee Bay made a good harbor, and Ohio wanted it, on general principles.

Then the affair began to get complicated. Congress accepted the new state with that constitution, but two years later declared that the southern boundary of the new Territory of Michigan would follow the old tip-of-Lake-Michigan line. This line was resurveyed, and it struck Lake Erie east of Maumee Bay, which of course meant that that river mouth belonged to Michigan. The few people who then lived in Michigan could not have cared less, but the people of Ohio cared a good deal, and they had their own survey made, establishing a line that put Maumee Bay back in Ohio. So there was a long, slightly wedge-shaped bit of land from eight to ten miles wide, with survey monuments along each side, running from Lake Erie all the way to the Indiana line, and this long piece of ground was claimed by both states. It was governed according to the laws of Michigan Territory, but that made little difference, because there was nobody in it and consequently nothing to govern.

Now suddenly the business became of high importance to everybody. Michigan was being settled, and a good many of the settlers were coming in along or across the strip, so Michigan wanted full title to it. The port at Toledo was obviously going to be important, what with the constant rise in lake traffic, so Ohio wanted full title; wanted it all the more because it was projecting a canal to connect the Maumee with the Ohio River. To complicate matters still further, Michigan just now began to undergo a self-inflicted change in government, which might or might not be legal.

When Cass left office as governor of Michigan Territory, President Jackson appointed John T. Mason to succeed him, and Mason installed his son, twenty-year-old Stevens T. Mason, as territorial secretary. A short time afterward, the older Mason got tired of Michigan, resigned, and went somewhere west; and his youthful son, who had not resigned as secretary, became acting governor under the law. Since he was not yet twenty-one, he became mildly famous as "the Boy Governor"—a situation President Jackson soon remedied by naming George B. Porter, a politically prominent Pennsylvania lawyer, as the new governor. Now, in July 1834, just as the border dispute was coming to a head, Porter unexpectedly died, and the Boy Governor was Boy Governor again.

Mason started out in a pacific vein, advising the legislative council not to take any drastic action on the territorial dispute, because that was something Michigan and Ohio could easily settle, between them, once Michigan became a state. This, Mason believed, would be soon, and when a territorial census showed that Michigan now had 85,000 inhabitants —substantially above the legal minimum for statehood—he believed the time had arrived. He argued that the famous ordinance of 1787 that set up the Northwest Territory made statehood automatic, once the population level was right, so he proceeded to call a convention to make a constitution for the state of Michigan. He believed it was up to him to act as state governor while this was going on, and he also believed in acting vigorously.

So when Governor Lucas of Ohio claimed jurisdiction over the disputed strip and organized it formally as an Ohio county, Governor Mason countered by ordering the arrest of any outsiders (meaning Ohioans) who accepted office or behaved like office-holders in this inalienable section of southern Michigan. Now Michigan and Ohio began to bristle at each other in earnest, or at least in what looked like earnest. Militia companies were mobilized, peace officers were sworn in, and up and down the strip there was defiant oratory, much of it in bar-rooms, and much impromptu parading and chest thumping. The Ohio legislature voted $300,000 to enforce Ohio's claim; Michigan's territorial legislative council countered by appropriating $315,000. Flags were put up on poles and hauled down by parties in opposition. An officer of Ohio militia, one B. F. Stickney, was arrested by Michigan deputies, and one of his sons set out to rescue him. Stickney had two sons, and in some fit of backwoods eccentricity, he had given them numbers rather than names: they were, in order of seniority, One Stickney and Two Stickney. One was peaceful, but Two Stickney went on the warpath and wounded a deputy sheriff with a pen-knife—which seems a wholly inappropriate weapon for a frontier brawl—and then fled to deepest Ohio, where Michigan could not follow him.

All of this, of course, had resounding echoes in Washington, where Jackson's attorney general confided to the president that, legally, Michigan seemed to have a good case. All very well:

but a presidential election was coming up soon, and Ohio had a full-sized Congressional delegation, two active senators, and a substantial number of voters who must not be antagonized. (Michigan, as a mere territory, did not need such careful handling.) In the spring of 1835, Jackson sent out commissioners to make a peaceful settlement; failed, when Mason agreed to refrain from the use of force only on condition that Lucas kept his minions out of the disputed strip, which Lucas flatly refused to do. In the end, Jackson notified Mason that he would be removed from office if he actually arrested any Ohio officials. Mason ignored this and arrested nine of them (including, one supposes, the parent of indomitable Two Stickney). Meanwhile, the Michigan convention presented a state constitution, and a Democratic convention, convening shortly thereafter, nominated Stevens Mason for governor of the new state; at about which time Andrew Jackson, who believed in firm discipline for recalcitrant states, removed Mason from office. A presidentially appointed successor freed the arrested Ohioans, the people of Michigan elected Mason governor and sent two senators and a representative to Washington, and announced that they had a state and not a territory.

Partly right, partly wrong. Congress worked out a plan: the faraway, bleak, little-known upper peninsula would be added to Michigan if Michigan would give up all claim to the Toledo strip. Indignantly, the Michigan legislature rejected this scheme, declaring the upper peninsula was sterile, snowbound, and destined to remain a wilderness. So, officially, Michigan was a sovereign state out of the Union, and it would have to remain so until the Congressional plan was accepted.

So here was a complete lawyer's nightmare, with clouded titles and disputed authority running all along the border and a new state existing in limbo. How long this would have gone on is beyond telling . . . but a lucky accident occurred, and suddenly everything was settled. The United States Treasury contained a surplus, and this was going to be distributed to the states, pro rata; if Michigan were a state, she would receive $400,000, but if she did not become a state immediately, that money would be gone forever. The elected representatives, unofficial spokesmen, and every-day people of Michigan realized that the upper peninsula after all had great attractions and would some day undoubtedly be most valuable . . . and without much loss of time, the deal was accepted, the claim to the Toledo strip was abandoned once and for all, and in January 1837, Michigan became a full-fledged state in the Union, both peninsulas together.

Meanwhile, as the great reconciliation was being made, the Erie and Kalamazoo Railroad completed its line to Adrian, and there was a big celebration when a team of horses pulled the first car into town. Sometime in the spring of 1837, a steam locomotive, shipped to Toledo by boat, went puffing out along the track at a top speed of possibly ten miles an hour, and the first steam-powered railroad west of the Alleghenies was in operation.

6

A Right to Expect Much

ROM this distance, it almost seems that the first railroad, the modest little Erie and Kalamazoo, whose thirty miles managed to represent everything that lay ahead, simply added to Michigan's problems. It was slow, rickety, dangerous, faintly ridiculous, and altogether primitive. However, Michigan itself was primitive, and as it moved from one era to another, it needed fluidity of movement more than it needed anything else; conquering the wilderness was work enough by itself, without wasting any muscle on the mere business of getting to the site of the job. And so the railroad implanted one desire that had extensive consequences. More than a century afterward, William S. Knudsen, president of General Motors, remarked that the American is a person who insists on going from Point *A* to Point *B,* sitting. This characteristic goes 'way back. The early railroads started it.

The first passengers on this railroad did not always sit. The track had excessive grades and the locomotives lacked power, and on up-hill drags the passengers often had to get out and walk, counting themselves lucky if they were not actually obliged to push. The chains that bound the carriages together had too much slack, and when the train began to move it went with a series of neck-snapping jerks; the smokestack sent out live embers from the cord wood that went into the firebox, and those who rode on top of the carriages (which were made like conventional stage coaches, in the beginning) got holes burned in their clothes. Every so often, the strap iron that was fastened on top of the wooden rails came loose and sent vicious curling ends up through the floors of the cars, and not infrequently passengers were killed by them. At one time, early on, the railroad put into service a freakish car with a peaked roof, gothic windows and a central compartment that was higher than the ends, looking to modern eyes a bit like a cross between a corn crib and a split-level ranch house. It was unquestionably top-heavy, although because the trains ran so slowly it probably was not really very dangerous. It just looked odd, and before long it was retired.

But all of the defects that can be laid to the early railroads made very little difference. Americans will pay any price at all for faster transportation, and if it turns out to be dangerous, they think nothing of it. The railroads had horrifying wrecks; the early steamboats blew up with frightening regularity; when airplanes came in, they had a way of nose-diving into hillsides with the loss of all hands; and the automobile introduced itself with an annual death toll that is still astounding. None of this ever made the slightest difference. If occasional disasters are the price of rapid movement, the price will be paid without the slightest demur.

Actually, this is not the half of it. Every means of transportation, once adopted, imposes itself on society and exacts a price that nobody ever bargained for. As it becomes dominant, it compels the society that uses it to conform to its own special demands. Society carries its carriers, and it becomes what the bearing of this heavy load makes it. Having understood from the beginning that nothing needs to stay in place—indeed, that nothing should be allowed to stay in place, once it has served its immediate purpose—we cheerfully build ourselves around successive transportation systems and make whatever adjustments seem necessary.

So Michigan's early railroads were happily accepted with all of their imperfections, and the people wanted to have many more of them. A number of charters had been issued, but hardly any actual building was going on; and in 1837, the legislature got busy. Reflecting that the state constitution approved action on internal improvements to roads, canals, and navigable waters, the legislature ordained that the state should build three railroads across the lower peninsula—the Michigan Southern, following the Old Sauk Trail; the Michigan Central, running from Detroit to the Kalamazoo valley and then on to the mouth of the St. Joseph; and the Michigan Northern, which was to go from the St. Clair River to the mouth of the Grand River. There were also to be two cross-state canals and another one around the rapids of the St. Mary's River, at the Soo. It seemed logical to have the state do this building; after all, it built ordinary roads, so why should it not build railroads? They were simply pathways along which wheeled vehicles could be moved. Work was begun on the first two railroads, contracts were signed for the canals, and with boom times flourishing, the authorities undertook to speed the progress of practically everything with a strong dose of inflation.

When the state entered the Union, it contained fifteen chartered banks, all of them authorized to issue paper money— backed, of course, by ample reserves of specie, or hard money, by which the notes could be redeemed on demand. Now a new banking act was passed, which in effect allowed practically any solvent group of citizens to organize a new bank and issue paper currency. This seemed like a conservative step; a bank's organizers must pledge enough real estate to guarantee the security of its notes, and in addition must keep in the vaults enough specie to redeem 30 percent of the notes' value on demand. The authorities sat back to see what would happen.

A great deal happened, and it happened rather fast. The boom times that were in effect involved real estate, first and foremost, and groups of speculators were busy laying out future cities in the most unlikely places, printing tasty brochures showing hotels, docks, factories and acres of pleasant homes where nothing really existed except sand dunes and woods. Each group that operated thus could found a bank now, issue paper money, go to the land office and use that money to buy more government land, and intensify the entire process. The kind of rising spiral that forms a tornado picked up speed enormously.

A great many people, obviously, lost a good deal of money through the activities of the real estate speculators; but the point to bear in mind—now that all of the losers and all of the losses have gone beyond recall—is that the settlers in this new state were subject to runaway optimism, not because of villainous promoters, but because they actually could see a new world taking shape before them. The limited, pinched world all men were used to was being rolled up like a scroll, and something new was being brought forth. Here was a land in which all old rules, seemingly, were off. Anything could happen and people did not really need the sharp prod of inflation to see gaudy visions.

In 1831, before the dizzy spiral even began, the French traveler Alexis de Tocqueville, visiting in Detroit, wanted to see nature in the wild and was taken to the Saginaw River, to a trading post right where the city of Saginaw is now. Looking about him, he had reflections which he wrote down thus:

> In a few years these impenetrable forests will have fallen; the sons of civilization and industry will break the silence of the Saginaw; its echoes will cease; the banks will be imprisoned by quays; its current which now flows on unnoticed and tranquil through a nameless waste, will be stemmed by the prows of vessels. More than a hundred miles sever the solitudes from the great European settlements, and we are perhaps the last travelers allowed to see its primitive grandeur.[1]

Seven years later, when the boom was going full tilt, Henry Schoolcraft, commissioner of Indian affairs, visited the tiny Lake Michigan seaport of Grand Haven and took passage upriver in the sternwheeler *Washtenong* to Grand Rapids, a village dominated chiefly by the trader Louis Campau. Schoolcraft, a scholarly man committed to his work with the Indians, was no more on the make than was Tocqueville, but when he looked about him in this clearing in the wilderness he saw just what Tocqueville had seen, and he wrote it down:

> The fall of Grand river here creates an ample water power; the surrounding country is one of the most beautiful and fertile imagin-

---

1. Fuller, *Historic Michigan*, I:285.

able, and its rise to wealth and populousness must be a mere question of time, and that time hurried on by a speed that is astonishing. This generation will hardly be in their graves before it will have the growth and improvement which in other countries are the result of centuries.[2]

People saw things so then, and what they saw colored what they did and what they wanted, and perhaps, at last, what they became. The shapes painted on clouds by released desire overlapped the hard reality of what had to be, and sober men looked for more than they were likely to get. Lewis Cass, trying to tell his fellows that the Indians were people to be helped and protected, said of them: "They have a right to expect much." [3] Everybody had that right, and exercised it, and all we can say now is that the bubble finally broke and let daylight in on a landscape that had been unreal and significant.

The man who stuck the sharp point of a knife into the bubble was, of course, President Andrew Jackson, who had his own ideas about bankers. Michigan was not the only state whose banks were emitting bank notes that had nothing in particular to stand on, and Jackson presently issued what was known as his "specie circular," which said that from now on people who bought land from the United States government had to pay for it in gold or silver—hard cash, and no bank notes. There was a minor exception: bona fide settlers could go on using notes for four months, provided that they bought no more than 320 acres of land, but the speculators were out, and the party was over.

Tight money, in other words; for protection, a quickly passed state law suspending specie payments. (In simple language, a man holding bank notes could no longer take them to the bank that printed them and get hard cash for them.) It was felt that the squeeze would soon be over; if people would just be patient a little while, confidence would be restored, and the spiral could go on again. This was a vain hope, to be sure, because instead of getting better, things got ever so much worse, but so much

2. Fuller, *Historic Michigan*, I:285.
3. Frank B. Woodford, *Lewis Cass, the Last Jeffersonian*, in May and Brinks, *A Michigan Reader*, p. 179.

wind had been generated that the boom was carried on for a time faster than ever. Taking advantage of the new rule, banks sped more notes into circulation and the real estate wizards performed ever more elaborate incantations. A young woman from New York whose husband had been talked into investing in some future metropolis of Michigan left a canny account of the kind of operations she beheld:

> When lots were to be sold the whole fair dream was splendidly emblazoned on a sheet of super-royal size; things which only floated before the mind's eye of the most sanguine were portrayed with bewitching minuteness for the delectation of the ordinary observer. Majestic steamers plied their paddles to and fro upon the river; ladies crowding their decks and streamers floating on the wind. Sloops dotted the harbors, while noble ships were seen in the offing. Mills, factories and lighthouses—canals, railroads and bridges, all took their appropriate positions. Then came the advertisements, choicely worded and carefully vague, never setting forth any thing which might not come true at some time or other, yet leaving the buyer without excuse if he chose to be taken in.[4]

All things come to an end sooner or later, and the end of this sort of business finally arrived. Prices began to drop, and then fell as if they had gone over a cliff, and the real estate that was pledged to support all those slips of green paper went down and kept on going down, and in many cases became worth nothing at all. Now the notes had nothing to support them but the specie that law required the banks to have, and it developed that the bank commissioners had not always been alert. In many cases, the specie that new banks were required to have in their vaults consisted of kegs of nails, or rocks, or things equally indigestible; it was reported that one bank's assets consisted of a fine collection of millstones, grindstones, and whetstones, and there were instances where several banks collectively possessed a keg of real money that they passed back and forth when the bank examiners came around, so that all of them could look law-abiding. Before long, most of the gaudy new banks were hopelessly

4. Carolyn Kirkland, "A New Home—Who'll Follow," in *Michigan History,* XLII, no. 1:29.

bankrupt, and the notes they had sprayed across the state were worth nothing whatever. It came to be said that many of these banks were based on paper cities laid out in the dense forests where nobody lived but wildcats, and the term *wildcat bank* came into use.

So the party was over, and the price of collective gullibility victimized by chicanery was seen to be high. And yet it was not, at bottom, entirely a matter of fools set upon by knaves, even though foolishness and knavery did abound for a time. The lid had come off, in sober truth, and what Tocqueville and Schoolcraft had seen was precisely what the immigrants had glimpsed all the tortuous way to the wild land that was being turned into a garden. As Cass said of the Indians, these people had a right to expect much, and if they now expected that life somehow was going to be lived on a different basis hereafter, they were touching the edge of sober truth.

A new light was shining on the American landscape, most visible in the new country but perceptible everywhere, seen at times even in Europe. Until this generation, man thought he lived in an unchanging world in which his condition was fixed and his possibilities were limited. Now he was discovering that this notion was wrong. The whole point of the American experience (two centuries old, and more, by this time) was that there was going to be a great deal of change and that most of the accepted limits had vanished. The light by which this discovery was made had begun to glow in Virginia and Massachusetts and had grown immensely brighter at Philadelphia and Yorktown; and now, just as men were beginning to see that they could make of themselves what they chose, they found themselves looking at an uncovenanted abundance of natural resources—and this, too, when the developing industrial revolution needed precisely that sort of abundance in order to realize its own limitless potential.

In 1634, Jean Nicolet, going through the wilderness in his quest for furbearing animals or for good routes from the Straits to the out-back, noted that there were great forests with many tall pines in them along the Muskegon River, longest in the peninsula. He was not especially interested, and neither was anybody else, and in 1812, when a trading post was established there, no one gave the trees a thought. Now, in 1836, as the Ionia land office opened all of this land for purchase, some bright person looked at the pines and had a thought; and in 1837, a sawmill was put at the mouth of the Muskegon, and Michigan's great lumber era began.

Two things are to be remembered in connection with this.

The first is that, until the late 1830s, there was no reason for anyone to grow excited about pine trees in Michigan because nobody wanted to buy them. The eastern country was getting its pine lumber from Maine in vast quantities, with more to come from Pennsylvania and up-state New York, and the western country had not yet reached the point where it needed to bring in much lumber from outside. But now the prairies were beginning to be developed, and there were unending acres of good farm land that did not contain enough trees to build a cowshed. Chicago was being born, and it was about to grow prodigiously, reflecting the runaway growth of the whole Illinois country, and almost overnight there was a lusty market with what looked like an insatiable demand for building lumber. The tall, straight pines made the best building lumber on earth, straight-grained, easy to work, light in weight but strong enough to make good houses and barns and factory buildings; and just at this moment, men who looked about them saw the pines on the Muskegon, not to mention the pines on the immense web of the Saginaw River system, not to mention the fringes of the unwelcome upper peninsula, not to mention still other places that nobody but a few superannuated fur traders knew about. The boom was on.

The other thought to bear in mind is that there were two Michigans. One of them was ready to blossom out with wheat fields and corn fields and good flocks fattening on lush pastures, and with bustling cities born of the soil's richness, just as soon as industrious men cleared away the cover and broke the ground to the plow. The other Michigan, comprising a good two thirds of the lower peninsula and nearly all of the upper peninsula, was valuable for the trees it bore (and also, all unsuspected, for the minerals it sometimes contained), but aside from this it was hardly worth anything. Much of it simply could not be farmed at all, and hardly any of it could be farmed at a profit. But the way this second Michigan was treated was a direct consequence of the program that had done so well with the first Michigan.

It was entirely natural, for instance, for the people of this state to think that the enormous forest ought to be cut down as rapidly as possible; take away trees, and you create good farming country, and the smiling agricultural belt that stretched away from Lake Erie to the lower part of Lake Michigan would be duplicated all the way to the Straits, and beyond. The trees were simply in the way. The fact that the pines could be reduced to boards and sold at a good profit was simply an unexpected bonus—delightful, of course, but really beside the point. All experience indicated that to slash away at the wilderness and destroy its trees mercilessly was nothing more than ordinary prudence. Besides, John Jacob Astor and his confreres had set the pattern, with the fur trade: take what there is, take all of it, and take it as fast as you can, and let tomorrow's people handle tomorrow's problem.

So the state began to get at its pine forests. At first, it did little more than nibble at them. There was this mill at the mouth of the Muskegon; there had been a little sawmill near Port Huron for many years, cutting lumber to meet the modest needs of Detroit; and when Schoolcraft visited the rapids of the Grand River, men were preparing to harness the waterpower there to cut lumber. Downstream, by the big lake, the settlement of Grand Haven had been founded, and people were under contract to bring logs down to a new mill. Here and there, all along the shores of Lake Huron and Lake Michigan, there were places where a few men cut and stacked hardwood to fuel the steamboats, and towns that were to have high times as lumber towns began modestly by selling firewood. In some places, the fishing was better business than lumbering. Alpena, which was to have a great future in lumber, started life as a modest fishing port, with a little whiskey-for-furs trade with the resident Indians as a sideline; and Menominee, which built a sawmill as early as 1832 and was to become the greatest lumber port of the upper peninsula, found during its early years that the biggest returns came from whitefish and lake trout.

But the demand for white pine lumber kept on growing, and Michigan suddenly found itself in the lumber industry right up to the neck. It drew a number of lumbermen from the state of Maine—significantly, an early settlement near the great lumber port of Bay City was named Bangor—and it discovered that French Canadians, used to the wilderness and agile as cats, were first-rate men with the axe and peavey. And as the business grew, with places like Saginaw and Muskegon building vast sawmill principalities, a new profession developed and became essential to the industry's operation. The hungry mills, it was discovered, could not exist without the services of the land-looker, also known as the timber cruiser. Before the pine trees could be cut down, somebody had to go and find them.

This seems odd, in view of all that has been said and written about the boundless forests of Michigan's pines, but the long years have given a faulty picture. There were places, to be sure, where pines and nothing but pines lay across the hills like lake-to-lake carpeting, but the country was totally lacking in roads, towns, and reliable word-of-mouth reports, and these places were not as easy to find as a resident of today's explicitly mapped country might suppose. Furthermore, they were not characteristic. Mostly, the pines were part of a great mixed forest that contained large numbers of maples, beeches, elms, and oaks, along with hemlocks and balsam firs. Sometimes the pines would grow side by side with these other trees, and sometimes they would stand in separate belts or clusters, surrounded by them—encircled by cedar swamps, as likely as not, or by a tangle of birch and aspen and tamarack. To discover them could take a weary amount of tramping up hill and down dale in all weathers, and involved an intimate acquaintance with such maddening pests as mosquitoes, no-see-ums, and deer flies.

Simply discovering these stands of pine was only the beginning. They had to be precisely located by the surveyor's grid, so that the man who proposed to buy them could go to the land office, pay his money, and know that he had obtained exactly the land he wanted. This meant that the land-looker had to carry a compass, know about the surveyor's trade, locate the hidden markers and witness trees, and possess the knack of measuring distances accurately simply by tramping over them—hard enough at any time, almost impossible when it involved crossing a rocky ravine and plowing through a tangle of down timber left by some forgotten tornado. A secondary problem here was that yellow jackets made a practice of nesting in these horrid broken thickets, and the man who crossed one was almost certain to step into such a nest, every so often. Another secondary problem was that the man who did all of this hiking lived on slender rations; he ate what he carried with him, for the most part, because he had very little time for hunting and fishing while he worked and no desire at all to carry any more equipment than was absolutely necessary. If he really wanted to travel light, as most timber-cruisers did, he carried salt pork, hard tack, and tea. After a couple of weeks, one gathers that this became somewhat monotonous.

Finally, the land-looker had to know what he was seeing. The pines would probably be mixed in the hardwoods, which at that stage of the industry's development were worthless. How many hardwoods were in the mixture? If there were too many, or if the pines were under-sized, cutting the tract would not pay, so it was by no means enough for the cruiser to come back and report that such-and-such a tract contained a good growth of pine; he had to be able to submit an informed estimate of the number of board feet of sawed lumber that would come out of an acre of that tract's land, and the estimate had to be tolerably accurate.

On top of everything else, the timberland had to be accessible, which meant that the trees that were to be cut down had to be situated reasonably close to a river. "Reasonably close" meant within two or three miles. At that stage of the game, there were no railroads in the pine country, and no highways worth mentioning, and if the felled trees could not be floated to the sawmill, they could not be taken out at all. That is why the first mills grew up at the mouths of the rivers. They not only had to have access to deep water, so that steamboats and schooners could come in and pick up the finished lumber; they had to get their raw material—logs, the awkwardest raw material to handle any factory owner ever saw—by water or they would not get it at all. It ought to be added that, when the trees were felled and cut up into logs, the logs were moved to the riverside by sleigh, in winter-time, because it was only on roads of glare ice that land transportation was possible; and this meant that, between the place where the trees were felled and the nearest river, there could not be any up-hill stretches.

All in all, then, the land-looker had a demanding job. One of its problems was that, when he got into a dense forest—and all the Michigan forest was dense, in those days, because it was all primeval wilderness—it was almost impossible for him to see any distance at all, and he could easily go within two hundred yards of a fine stand of pines without knowing it. If he could come out on a hill and shin up a tree he might get a look around, but that was not always possible; and when it was, it did not always work. One recourse the wise old-timer had was simply to stand still and listen. Mature pines gave themselves away; if there was the least breath of air stirring, their upper branches whispered together—a faint, unforgettable rustling sound, wholly unlike the noise made by any other trees. Over and over again a veteran timber-cruiser got into a good stand of pine just by following his sense of hearing.

Once you got into it, a pine forest was impressive. Mature white pines went up straight, from 125 to 175 feet high, and for the first two thirds of their growth they had no branches: there were just those rows of tall, gently-tapering dark gray columns, bearing the green branches that suicidally betrayed themselves in the breeze, cutting off the sunlight except for small golden bits that dropped down from the green canopy overhead. In many cases, this perpetual twilight checked the growth of smaller trees, so that there was hardly any underbrush. The biggest, straightest trees were known to the lumbermen as "cork pine," the wood was so light and buoyant; put the logs in the river, and they would float right on the surface, able to glide over shoals and snags that would stop logs more deeply submerged. Looking at a stand of trees, the timber-cruiser would jot down his estimate: "Five log pines, with ten percent uppers." [5] This meant that five average pine logs from these trees would provide a thousand board feet of sawed lumber, and of quality high enough so that at least 10 percent of it would be altogether free of knots or other blemishes.

Having found his pines, the cruiser then had to fix their exact location with respect to the surveyor's grid: he had to be able to measure distances and form precise angles, so that he could say that he wanted half a square mile of this land described in terms such as these: "The southwest quarter of section 9 of township 11 north, range 13 west"—with notes separately recorded, telling what watercourse was available and where it led. And then, of course, he had to get to the nearest land office and get the land recorded and paid for. Occasionally, this involved racing with some other land-looker who had his eye on the same plot of ground. The average land-looker, by the way, was a free lance, who scouted out pine for mill owners down-state; at the same time, he would usually do a little buying on his own account, so that he was led on not merely by the prospect of a fee, but also by the profit motive, as well. If he struck it rich for the firm that hired him, he might also strike it rich for himself.

One fabulous timber-cruiser race took place in the spring of 1854, when a man named David Ward located a fine stand of cork pine far up between the headwaters of the Manistee and Au Sable rivers, which was a long, long way from anywhere at all, in those days. Ward understood that the agent for a rival lumberman named Addison Brewer was also looking at this same stand of pine, and he understood that, once he had the data he needed, he had better get back to the land office just as quickly as possible. The nearest office, as it happened, was at Ionia, but that was "near" only in a manner of speaking, and, anyhow, Ward could not go there directly; he had first to visit his principals in Detroit and get the cash and vouchers with which he could validate his claims when he got to the land office. So he shouldered his pack and set out to hike—somehow, the word seems inadequate—eighty miles overland to the Tobacco River,

5. William Davenport Hulbert, *White Pine Days on the Taquamenon* (Lansing: Historical Society of Michigan, 1949), p. 10.

where he picked up a canoe and paddled eighty more miles down-river to Saginaw, whence he was able to go by stage and railroad to Detroit. There he got his money, hired a horse and buggy, and drove to Lansing, an eighteen-hour pull, and at Lansing he caught a stage to Ionia. There, at last, he registered his claim. Before the day ended, Brewer's agent showed up, losing by three or four hours in a race that had lasted more than a week.

Much like this was the race won by William Callam, a bright young lumber camp foreman who worked in the Saginaw Valley some years after Ward's exploit. Callam discovered a magnificent stand of cork pine up the Chippewa River, checked at the land office and learned that it had never been sold, quit his job, got an outfit, and went up to give it a close examination. It was great stuff, three-log pine, with "uppers" which, it finally turned out, were worth more than three times as much as run-of-the-mill timber. He measured, paced, and studied, and listed a number of forty-acre tracts that were fairly begging to be bought—and then one day discovered footprints in the matted duff beneath the trees: another timber cruiser was on the job! Callam shouldered his pack and set out for Saginaw, sixty miles away. According to legend, which is probably true, he made it without stopping to sleep, tottered into his home at Saginaw just long enough to scoop up his savings from a hiding place in his bedroom, and then got down to the land office. (By this time there was one in Saginaw.) There, he made out the papers, paid in the money, and was just pocketing the receipt that confirmed his title when the other land-looker came in.

Whether you won those races or lost them, you at least had an active life, all the way.

The emphasis throughout the story of the lumber boom—which grew so great that outlanders came to think of Michigan as one great lumber camp—was on the need for transportation. This was not only needed by the men who raced one another to the land office; it was needed even more desperately by the boss lumbermen themselves, because, at bottom, the lumber industry was mostly a matter of moving timber from the place where the trees grew to the distant yards where contractors wanted to buy boards. Finding the trees, cutting them down, and sawing out the planks were fairly simple—well, *fairly* simple: it was carrying the stuff that raised the problems. And just when the state was feeling obliged to build railroads to meet the needs of farmers, settlers, and merchants, it began also to feel obliged to meet the needs of the lumber industry, too. This industry became almost incredibly big. It has been estimated that in the sixty years beginning in 1847, when the boom really got started, the value of Michigan's lumber output was at least a billion dollars greater than the value of all the gold dug in California in the same time. When an industry that big put on pressure for a proper railroad network, the pressure was bound to be noticed.

From the moment it became a state, Michigan had been enthusiastic about railroads, and its leap into railroad construction—energetically pushed by Governor Mason, who had been elected in his own right after his ins and outs as territorial governor—had involved a $5,000,000 bond issue. This was duly floated, and work on the Central and Southern railroads began, and the young governor reflected that, when Congress offered Michigan the upper peninsula in return for the Toledo strip, it promised, as an added sweetener, to pay the state 5 percent of the net proceeds from the sale of public lands. For a short time, everything looked fine, and then the sky turned very dark indeed. The real estate boom burst, most cruelly; all of those wildcat banks blew up, the state was flooded with completely worthless paper currency, and sales of government land in Michigan dropped from more than 5,000,000 acres in 1836 to a scant 175,000 acres in 1839. The Central and Southern railroads, built as far as Jackson and Hillsdale, respectively, operated at a profit, but made just about half enough to meet the interest charges on the big bond issue. The across-Michigan canals languished and died, and the canal that was to by-pass the rapids at the Soo perished of what can only be called co-operative malnutrition.

Which is to say that the state appropriated money for the Soo Canal, set up a commission to supervise the job, and signed up with a contractor to do the building. The contractor went to the spot, mustered a crew of diggers, and discovered that the plan as set forth would require him to dig across the Fort Brady reservation, where there was a spillway bringing down water to operate a government mill. Army authorities notified him that he must under no circumstances violate the integrity of the government reservation or cut across the spillway; and when he brought his diggers to the scene, a platoon of infantry in full regalia met him and compelled him to go away. There was a great carrying-on, and the state of Michigan and the United States government exchanged furious words for quite a time, and no canal was dug or even started. The state seemed about to proceed against the contractor for failing to do his job, then got on his side and denounced Washington for not letting him do it, and in the end the whole flap died down, the canal remained an idea and nothing more, and the spillway to the government mill was not molested. It is just possible for a suspicious person to suspect that the whole business was a put-up job, with the contractor happy to get out of what he could see was going to be a losing contract, with the army willing to oblige him by lining up troops across the right of way, and with the state—deep in trouble, now, with actual bankruptcy threatened because of the overblown public transportation program—happy enough to forget about the whole matter.

Governor Mason, unfortunately, lost everything—his enthusiasm, his popularity, and, finally, his job. He had caused his state to bite off much more than it could chew, and when the whole business exploded, he got all of the blame. The Democratic party refused to renominate him when his term expired; in 1840, the state installed a Whig governor; and Mason dropped entirely out of sight, victim of one of the immutable rules of American politics: office-holders identified with expanding hopes cannot be re-elected in a depression. The one thing everyone understood was that the state ought to get out of the railroad business, and in a short time it did so, selling the Central and the Southern roads for what it could get, which turned out to be about $860,000 less than the cost of construction to date. The voters did not want to get burned again, and, when they adopted a new constitution in 1850, they put in a clause forbidding the state to put any money, ever again, in any railroad enterprise.

As a matter of fact, the state sold out just when the two roads were beginning to be prosperous, although whether the state could have cashed in on the opportunities if it had kept its ownership is probably a question. Incomplete as they were, the Michigan Central and the Michigan Southern were carrying increasing numbers of passengers and increasing amounts of freight. Settlers were coming in again, and the produce of the new farms was beginning to call for transportation; furthermore, Chicago was suddenly becoming an incomprehensible, booming place that created traffic and created railroads, so that these two lines forgot about the original plan to get across the lower peninsula to blue water and drove furiously down to get out of Michigan and into Chicago. (Lines owned and operated by the state probably could not legally have built across the state line.) The demand for quicker means of getting from here to there was becoming more and more strident.

What would have looked like unbelievable speed, two decades earlier, was now inadequate. In 1838, Governor Mason had to go to New York to arrange for that unhappy bond issue. Returning, with a trunk containing $110,000 in cash, he wanted to make the trip as short as possible, so he went thus: from New York to Albany, by Hudson River steamboat; from Albany to Utica, by railroad; from Utica to Syracuse, by stagecoach; from Syracuse to Oswego, by canal boat; from Oswego to the mouth of the Niagara River, by steamboat; from that point to Buffalo, by railroad—and from Buffalo to Detroit, at last, by steamboat. That was the best anyone could do just then, but in five more years it would be utterly out of date.

Similarly with the trip from Detroit to Chicago. Just before the state sold itself out of the railroad business, people were marveling that it took less than forty-eight hours to make that trip. One went by Michigan Central to Jackson, 80 miles in six hours, covered the 120 miles to St. Joseph by stage coach in twenty-six hours, and then got on a steamer for a seven-hour run across 69 miles of lake to Chicago. A few years earlier, this would have seemed marvelously speedy; now it was slow, and it was also uncomfortable—no one who could avoid it endured a 120-mile trip by stage, and the ride over the rails as far as Jackson was a jolting, start-and-stop affair whose chief virtue was that the passengers at least never had to get out and push. In 1849, the railroad got through as far as New Buffalo, at the mouth of the Galien River; and for three or four years, that became the jumping-off point for Chicago, with three side-wheel steamboats in service, and with the railroad boasting that it carried 100,000 passengers in one year's time. Finally, in 1852, both railroads got into Chicago, and rail service between Chicago and Detroit was unbroken.

Surest sign of changing times actually came a few years before this. In 1839, some enterprising steamboat man in Buffalo began advertising pleasure cruises, fifteen-day round trips between Buffalo and Chicago, catering, not to emigrants nor to business men, but simply to people who wanted to enjoy two weeks on the water. The boat carried a band, it picked up passengers at Cleveland and Detroit, and one happy traveler wrote of the beauty of the water which "as far as the eye can reach presents the most exquisite tints of the emerald, sparkling and leaping in the glad sunshine." [6]

6. H. A. Musham, "Early Great Lakes Steamboats," in *The American Neptune*, XVIII, no. 4:293.

7

Breakthrough at the Soo

𝒯OO much happened too fast. The several stages in the state's development were pressed together, so that past and future overlapped and obscured the present. The fur trade, born in the aboriginal wilderness, was still prospering while the state tried to bankrupt itself building railroads. Farmers were desperately burning forests just to get rid of them, while land-lookers were driving themselves to exhaustion finding new forests. And at the Soo portage, where no one had cared to make a canal, men laboriously inched small schooners and a little steamer or two up the long street and got them into Lake Superior, where there were no towns, hardly any people, and precious little freight, but where a tremendous possibility was beginning to be sensed. The mighty weight of the upper peninsula's copper and iron was beginning to exert pressure, even though hardly anyone knew where these things were or how much of them there might be.

Perhaps there was a dim awareness that the industrial age was about to break out of this wild, desolate, uninhabitable wilderness—wholly incongruous, as if Étienne Brulé should step up to shake hands with Henry Ford. Once again, what modern America had to have in unstinted plenty was waiting here in an abundance beyond anyone's dreams. After it was found and used, everything everywhere would be different.

But the setting was strange. The past was still here, and it was impossible to avoid looking at it. In the summer, the fur brigades came and went, as in the old days, and the Indians caught whole canoe-loads of whitefish at the rapids, while women boiled great iron kettles full of blackberries by the river bank to make jam. In the winter, time was frozen. A Presbyterian missionary in 1831 noted how the winter mails moved; two men on snowshoes drove dogs hitched to a toboggan, which carried a tent, blankets, food, and a bag of mail. They went forty-five miles to the Straits, crossed on the ice, and then went all the way down to Saginaw and Detroit through a cold, beautiful, and killing wasteland where blue shadows lay on the snow in the moonlight. In a month or two, they would come back with news from the outside.

The military garrison at Fort Brady had little to do and made the most of it. The missionary found, to his horror, that each soldier was issued one gill of whiskey per day. (One gill: four fluid ounces, a very solid shot.) In addition, each man was allowed to buy from the sutler, and the sutler reported that he sold about eighty gills every day—some of them, to be sure, to people who were not soldiers. The missionary organized a temperance society, and to everyone's surprise, got sixty soldiers to join it in short order, the number rising to seventy a week or so later. The captain in command, dazed and unbelieving, remarked that he had been in the army twenty years without seeing anything like this; his men had been the country's worst soldiers, he said, and now they were the best.

Counting Indians, soldiers, and white civilians, there were not very many people at the Soo in the 1830s, and there was not much for any of them to do; and as a matter of fact, they were waiting for something they sensed but hardly understood. The whole Lake Superior country was haunted, as a matter of fact. Far to the west, there was Isle Royale, a forty-five-mile-long slab of rock set off with fir trees and fringed by surf breaking on hidden reefs. Indians had visited this island many centuries before any white man had heard of America, mining copper there, taking it across Lake Superior in birchbark canoes, and then going Heaven knows where with the knives, spear-heads, and axes they made out of it. They left pits from which they had dug the copper, and stone hammers and fragments of poles used to pry the metal from the earth; and in one place, sixteen feet below ground level, a geologist found a great copper boulder weighing more than two tons, which the Indian miners had cut loose from the rock but which they were unable to bring to the surface. On the island, there was nothing to show that these prehistoric miners had built houses or towns: apparently, they simply camped there in the short summers and went away before the autumn storms came.

There were other diggings on the mainland, along the Keweenaw Peninsula and along the Ontonagon River, where Indians had mined copper, and the noteworthy thing was that here in the Lake Superior country—here only, in all places on earth—nuggets and chunks and globules of virgin copper were to be found in usable quantities. Stone-age man had stumbled into the age of metals without knowing what he was doing, had used the copper to make useful things, had sent these things off through whatever unimaginable trade channels may have existed five thousand years ago, and then had vanished utterly. When the first Frenchmen reached the upper lakes, no Indians they found knew anything about copper. The knowledge of it and the use of it had dropped out of knowledge.

So there were legends, the tales men tell themselves when they run into something they cannot explain. The Phoenicians had been here, back when Solomon's Temple was being built; or perhaps it was the Vikings, coming in Europe's dark ages, going into Hudson's Bay from Greenland and then dying here by the cold lake; or possibly the copper had been mined by the Aztecs, or, if not by the Aztecs, then by the Mound Builders, or maybe even by improbable people from the lost Atlantis. If none of this could be proved, or even supported by substantial evidence, nothing could exactly be disproved, either, and so the north country rested under a haze of enchanted imagination—a region everybody rather liked to hear about, but which hardly anybody ever bothered to visit. The state had not wanted this land, in the first place, and had taken it under duress; and nearly half a century later, when vast fortunes had been made along the south shore of Lake Superior, a young civil engineer helping to lay out a railroad in the center of the lower peninsula was given a little indoctrination by his superior. The man laid a map of the state on the table and drew a line across the lower peninsula, straight west from Bay City to Lake Michigan.

"South of this line," he said, "is Michigan, a good state. North of it to the Straits is timber or cut-over land with not much future. And north of the Straits is *Hell*." [1]

But early in the 1840s, not long after the attempt to create a canal had failed, people were coming up to the Soo looking for a way to get west on Lake Superior. Michigan was beginning to realize that there was a lot of copper up there in the land it had not asked for; in a clumsy, uninformed, and frequently fatal way, a big copper rush was beginning.

That there was copper there was not really news. The Jesuits had known about it, long ago; the British knew it; and shortly after Pontiac's war, a little colony went to the Keweenaw, found an outcropping of copper, and tried to mine it. Everything was against them, including the weather. The shaft they had sunk caved in, and when they sat down to spend the winter, they found a copper-country winter like nothing they had ever heard of before: deep snow, hideous cold, a complete lack of roads, towns, settlers, or game, no place to go, and no way to get there anyway. As soon as the ice left the big lake in the spring, they piled into their boats and got back to the Soo as fast as they could go. They wanted no more copper mining in the Lake Superior country.

Later, in 1820, Lewis Cass made a notable trip by canoe from Detroit to the source of the Mississippi, far away in Minnesota, and Schoolcraft went with him and wrote a well-publicized report on what had been discovered, and this report made it clear that there was copper to be had. It spoke of a huge boulder of pure copper found on the Ontonagon; and during the next decade or so, various people went in to see it and bought it from the Indians. (Apparently the Indians happily sold it to all comers, figuring that to do the white man in the eye was no

1. Henry E. Riggs, *The Ann Arbor Railroad 50 Years Ago* (Ann Arbor: The Ann Arbor Railroad Co., n.d.), p. 6.

more than fair.) In 1843, one man, with unimaginable effort, managed to get the thing onto a schooner, got it over to the Soo, took it down the portage and moved it finally to Detroit, where he charged admission to people who wanted to see it and eventually managed to sell it to the U.S. government, which ultimately gave it a home in the Smithsonian Institution. The boulder was a ten-day marvel, and its chief effect was to remind everybody that there was a great deal of copper in the copper country.

Somehow, the thing touched off excitement. Here was a land where pure copper lay around in nuggets and chunks, and a lucky finder could just pick it up and walk off with it. Copper was a precious metal, or a semiprecious metal—anyway, the government made small coins out of it—and obviously there were fortunes to be made. Exact details were given in a report made by Dr. Douglas Houghton, the state geologist, who casually added that the upper peninsula also seemed to contain iron. Clearly, the land was rich in metals; and before 1843 was out, the great copper rush was on.

There were very few commercial carriers on Lake Superior: just the modest fleet that had been hauled up over the portage, vessels of forty tons or less. These found themselves crowded with "prospectors" who wanted to get to the copper country right away, and they could not begin to carry all the people who wanted to go. The over-flow got Indians or French fur traders to carry them in batteaux or canoes, and before long they were scrambling about the Keweenaw Peninsula and up the banks of the Ontonagon just as if they were Argonauts on the Sacramento, fifteen years later.

Hardly a one of these people knew anything at all about mining, or even about copper. They utterly failed to understand that, although it was a useful metal, it was not nearly so valuable as they innocently supposed. They expected to find lumps of the stuff lying on the beaches or taking the shade on the banks of rivers, and although a very few did make such finds, they were no better off afterward than before. In gold-rush country, a man who found half a dozen fist-sized nuggets had made a rich strike; in copper country, he did not have enough to pay for his salt pork and hard tack. Gold was paid for in dollars, by the ounce; copper, in pennies, by the pound. No man could possibly carry out, on his back, enough copper to pay his expenses.

This was indeed the richest copper country ever yet discovered, but its riches were locked up. Copper in unalloyed form did exist here, but except for a few bits of "float" copper—the nuggets that got everybody so excited—at least 95 percent of it was embedded in a conglomerate of pebbly rock with globules of copper interspersed between the pebbles, or in hard rock containing cracks or pockets in which the copper was found. Extracting it would be a laborious process, calling for the investment of a good deal of money. Furthermore, the Keweenaw Peninsula was a long, long way from the market, and every ton of the extracted copper would have to be hauled over that portage at the Soo. As if these handicaps were not enough, the country had ceased to be Indian country only one year earlier, and it had not yet been surveyed. How could a man register his claim without a surveyor's grid to go by?

It was no place for innocents, in other words, and the innocents who swarmed up here got nothing for their pains. Some of them, in point of fact, did not survive the first winter, and coming and going in open boats along the southern shore of Lake Superior was no way to bid for a long life. Still, a few men who were adequately financed and knew something about geology and about the problems of mining copper were on the scene, hard at work; and in 1844, the government established an army post, Fort Wilkins, by the principal copper-rush settlement, Copper Harbor, up near the tip of the Keweenaw Peninsula. The government probably supposed it was putting these soldiers there to protect the miners from the Indians. The Indians, watching while the soldiers built a stout palisade around the fort, told one another this fence was to protect the soldiers from the miners, and a common wisecrack in Copper Harbor was that the purpose really was to protect the Indians from everybody else. Life in Copper Harbor was as rowdy as life usually is in mining camps, and the same was true of the other towns created by the boom, Ontonagon and Eagle Harbor, but nobody really needed much military protection; and when the

Civil War came along, the government quietly closed down Fort Wilkins and took its soldiers to more active scenes.

Meanwhile, the work of getting the land surveyed was pushed, with a dedicated official named William Burt in charge, running section lines and making notes on geological character- istics met along the way. Burt had invented a solar compass, very useful in this land where mineral deposits made the ordi- nary magnetic compass almost useless; and one day he noticed that a magnetic compass carried by an assistant was swinging its north needle around so that it pointed slightly south of west. He remarked that they would be helpless without his solar compass, and then suggested that the party look around and see what they could find. They found innumerable outcrops of iron ore; and no wonder, because they had stumbled into the great Marquette Range, one of the richest deposits in the entire peninsula. When Burt's report was published, people who were interested in such things realized that a great deal of money could be made up here by men who commanded enough capital and technical knowl- edge.

So the gold-rush types were shaken out, and the copper and iron of the upper peninsula were exploited by men who knew what they were doing and had the strength to do it. A good deal of Boston money went into the copper business, and by 1845 two copper mines were in production. Also, in that year, a party from Jackson, in the lower peninsula, came up to scout for copper, found a great vein of iron ore a few miles inland from the present site of the city of Marquette, decided that they were an iron mining company, and in 1846 began bringing ore to the surface. The Stone Age had lasted just about as long, here in the upper peninsula, as it lasted anywhere on earth, but when the age of metals came in, it came with a rush.

Shortly after this, the country at large, including the national government, began to see that something big was going on here. It understood clearly enough that the greatest ore deposits in the nation were here to be used, and it slowly came to realize that getting the metals out of the ground was not enough; they also had to be got out of the Lake Superior country and this process had better not be too expensive. The miners were facing what the down-state lumbermen were facing: the biggest problem of all was the transportation problem.

The Jackson group got some ore to the surface in 1846, and set out to get a sample of it to the furnaces at Jackson to see how good it was. Working together, a number of them back-packed 300 pounds of ore down to the mouth of the Carp River on Lake Superior and shipped it on to the Soo, where it was carted over the portage and loaded into a schooner for transfer to Detroit. It reached Jackson at last, and the miners learned that their furnaces could not handle it; these furnaces had been designed for the common "bog iron," and this Lake Superior ore was just too high-grade for them. It was nice to know that the ore was so good, of course, but its goodness did create problems.

Several things were tried in the next few years. Ore was packed in barrels for shipment, but this was slow, cumbersome, and expensive. Deck-loads on sailing vessels were tried, but the transfer problem at the Soo was insurmountable. Finally, in desperation, the miners set up small furnaces and forges near the mines, to make blooms and bar iron on the spot. There was no coal anywhere around, so these forges had to use charcoal, and gangs had to cut down large numbers of hardwood trees and build kilns to turn the chunks into charcoal. The copper mines had it a little better, because once the virgin metal was extracted from hard rock or conglomerate, it could be formed into bars, and these, although heavy, were handier for shipping. Even at best, however, the region was being choked by the transportation bottleneck at the Soo, and it was just as hard to get the necessary machinery and other equipment in as it was to get the metals out again. In effect, the whole mining industry, which was obviously poised for a grand take-off, was being operated on a cottage-industry, piece-work basis. Something had to be done.

Inevitably, the plan for a canal around the rapids at the Soo was revived. Michigan appealed to the federal government for help, and although some members of Congress felt that the Soo was an awfully long way off, the government finally agreed to turn over 750,000 acres of government land to finance the job.

(In the end, the pretense that this was Michigan's canal was abandoned, and the canal became a federal operation, as it is to this day.) The riches of the great fang of desolate rock on the shore of an ice-cold lake were at last to be exploited by men who understood what a dollar was worth.

Probably it is in character that the two men chiefly responsible for this grand culmination did not profit by it. Douglas Houghton, who always had a first-rate press and who somehow managed to touch off the big metal rush, did not live to see what came of it. In the fall of 1845, he sailed from Eagle Harbor in a Mackinaw boat, along with other men, to scout along the shore and pick up some other surveyors. Lake Superior is beautiful and evil, and you coast along its shores in autumn at your own risk. A storm came up, the boat was smashed on the rocks, and young Houghton was drowned, mourned by one and all, his body not recovered until spring. Burt, who actually had had more to do with finding and locating the values that other men prized so highly, never met with disaster; he just was not interested in turning what he knew into cash, and he grew old and died in bed, while cannier people took what he knew and became extremely wealthy. Michigan has had people like William Burt, and in an absent-minded way, it honors them, but they hardly ever get rich. It may or may not be significant that it was Burt who finally surveyed the route for the great Soo Canal.

As construction jobs go, this was not really prodigious. There is a twenty-foot drop from Lake Superior to the level of Lake Huron, and one good lock will do the trick. There is hard rock to cut through, but nothing that high explosives and steel tools cannot handle, and aside from the fact that the work crews found this terrible country to live in, when winter came, and suffered at least once from an outbreak of cholera, there was no special trouble.

Men who ought to have known better feared that those who planned the new canal were much too optimistic. E. B. Ward of Detroit was the lakes' chief steamboat magnate, just then, and he wrote anxiously to a Michigan Congressman protesting that the locks, planned to measure 350 feet in length by 70 in width, were much too large; 260 feet by 60 feet would be ample, because steamboats too large for such locks would be too big to get up the St. Mary's River, which had shallow places with hard-rock bottoms. It would take a great deal of money to dredge those shallows, "a work which is not likely to be undertaken during the present century." [2] Furthermore, the 750,000-acre land grant would not finance a large canal, because the land involved was all but worthless and would not sell for more than seventy-five cents per acre. With luck, the land grant just might pay for a small canal, but if the state tried to build the bigger one, the job probably would never be finished.

It was natural for Captain Ward to feel this way. The largest vessel in his fleet would fit nicely into a 260-foot lock, and a steamboat that large was actually a big one, as lake vessels went. What Captain Ward failed to see (and it is hard to blame him, all things considered) was that the game was about to be played by new rules. The interlake trade in iron ore was about to begin; the canal would make that trade great, and that trade would make the canal great, and nobody had ever imagined the scale on which things hereafter were going to be done.

Afterward, it was easy to see it. Without any canal, ore simply could not be shipped down to the industrial region that needed it. With a small canal, the system of making small blooms on the spot and sending bar iron down to the factories would probably have been continued, and the nation's iron and steel industry would have remained small; and world history during the next century would have been quite different. But as the canal was actually built, with the over-sized locks Captain Ward considered so impractical, it was obviously cheaper to send the ore down in bulk cargoes, and the bulkier the cargoes were, the cheaper the whole process became. What was done at the Soo pulled the ores out of the upper peninsula rocks like a gigantic magnet—at exactly the moment when the country's manifold necessities demanded more and ever more things made of iron and steel, from railroad rails and bridges and all kinds of machinery to great guns and armor for iron-clad warships. (The document signed at Appomattox became inevitable, once the

2. Fuller, *Historic Michigan*, I:449.

canal was opened.) As a result, it became necessary in a very few years to enlarge the over-sized locks again and again, and the shallow places in the St. Mary's were gouged out in short order, along with other shallow places far to the south in the St. Clair and Detroit rivers. One of the most fateful acts in American history was performed when the Sault Ste. Marie Canal was thrown open for service in 1855.

One small set of figures, to show what was beginning to happen: in that first year, 1855, ships passing through the canal carried 30,000 tons of freight, counting machinery and supplies shipped up to the iron and copper ranges along with the ore shipped out. By 1862, 115,000 tons of iron ore went down to the lower lakes, and the next year it was more than 270,000. In 1901, after the locks had been enlarged a second time, the amount was 25,000,000. Captain Ward, as competent a business man as the lakes country afforded, had turned out to be a terrible prophet, not because he lacked intelligence, but simply because neither he nor the other men who were industrializing this wilderness had any notion how fast the process was going to go, once it got started.

Naturally, the impact of this new way of getting ore to the blast furnaces was felt first of all up on the ranges. Marquette suddenly turned into a city—it had been nothing at all, previously—along with places like Negaunee and Ishpeming; cities and towns sprang up along the copper range, most notably Houghton and Hancock and Calumet, and it was obviously going to be necessary to build enough of a railroad to get the ores of the Marquette Range down to the docks. The day of the independent prospector who tried to make a strike and then hoped he could turn what he had found into cash was over; but out in the forests and swamps and stubby mountains of the country south of the Marquette Range, land-lookers were industriously doing their job, thinking about iron more than about lumber, but going about it very thoroughly. The builders of the canal were being paid off out of that land grant, a third of which was to come from upper peninsula land, and it presently developed that they were able to select lands that had inordinately rich deposits of iron ore.

What this meant was that the iron boom, already moving along rapidly, became self-accelerating; there just naturally was more iron ore up here than anyone had imagined, and suddenly that fatal Michigan word—*inexhaustible*—began to be heard. The copper was inexhaustible, and so was the iron, and so of course was the timber, and it was time for everybody to step up to the Lord's table and eat his fill, no matter how great his appetite. Here was a bounty that would never run thin, and some of the most passionate entrepreneurs who ever lived found themselves existing like the flowers of the field, taking no thought for the morrow because today was so wonderful. It developed mental attitudes that still exist.

High times on the mineral ranges had unexpected side effects. One was the naturalization in Michigan of a good part of the population of southwestern England's Cornwall: the "Cousin Jacks," as they became known, men who had been mining British copper back home since the days of the ancient Phoenicians and who came over now to get the ore out of the Keweenaw Peninsula. They lent their own flavor to the land, flecking the north country's speech with their own words and phrases, adding to its diet the rugged but nourishing Cornish pasty, going far underground to dig out the metal that was valued so highly in the Boston counting houses. Some of the Keweenaw shafts went down for more than a mile, with spurs running out under Lake Superior; a long, long way from daylight, but at least the copper mines did not generate explosive gases the way the coal mines did, so the perils of fire were small. Of course, accidents could happen, and an accident that far underground is nothing to take lightly.

Another by-product was the development of a brief cottage-industry sort of operation: the appearance, in small towns along the shores of Lake Michigan in the lower peninsula, of blast furnaces, making pig iron in places that produced neither iron ore, coal, nor limestone. These testified chiefly to the low cost of water transportation and to the unparalleled abundance of the hardwoods from which charcoal could be made. Along the south shore of the upper peninsula, on the little Bay de Noc, the town of Escanaba came into being, primarily as a lumber port, and it got a railroad that brought down ore from the Marquette and Menominee ranges. It was remarkably inexpensive to put this ore in a small steamer and ship it down to such a lakeside town as Frankfort, where limestone from the quarries at the upper end of the lower peninsula could be imported with equal cheapness and where unending quantities of charcoal could be cooked up out of the hardwood forests—which, as everyone knew, were inexhaustible. So, for several decades, many small lake-side towns had blast furnaces, turning out pig iron that was shipped to processors farther south. The Pennsylvania coke ovens finally put a check to this, and anyway the hardwood forests turned out to be exhaustible, after all; but for a time, the iron industry was spattered all around the fringes of the lumber country—one more example of industrialization coming in before the primeval wilderness had disappeared.

If the canal at the Soo had opened the high country to full development, it still was not a year-round operation. In December, the big lake froze, as did the lakes below it; the locks could not operate, and the St. Mary's River was sheathed in ice—and, in short, no steamships or schooners could move. Winter conditions lasted at least until April, often until May, and while they lasted, upper Michigan was back in the old days, locked in with its own loneliness, and the outside world a long way off. The quickest way out for people at Marquette or on the copper range was by snowshoe and dog sled, south to Green Bay, two hundred miles and below zero all the way; isolation was just about complete. Now and then, when bad weather delayed the arrival of the first ships in, come spring, there were hungry times. The appearance of the first ship from down below was always a big event. One of the things to remember about the north country in those days is that it produced just about no food at all. When winter came, people ate what they had stock-piled, or they did not eat.

The steamboats on which so much depended had themselves been changing. Until the 1840s, the Great Lakes steamboat was invariably a side-wheeler, chiefly because that was the way all steamboats were built then. The ungainly walking-beam engines that drove the paddle wheels were poorly developed in those days, and had a way of showing good power on the down stroke and very little on the up stroke, which meant that the boat tended to go in surges, a sort of lunge-and-pause arrangement which, when the boat encountered rough weather, made it remarkably easy for everyone aboard to get seasick. Even worse was the fact that boilers and engines had to be amidships and were very bulky, which meant that the best space in the ship could not be used for cargo. All in all, these side-wheelers were not well adapted for the carriage of bulk freight, which was just the kind of freight the mineral ranges were offering.

Fortunately, in 1841, a new sort of steamer appeared—the *Vandalia*, built in Oswego, New York, to trade with Chicago via the Welland Canal, which made it possible for comparatively small vessels to go from Lake Ontario to Lake Michigan without a break. *Vandalia* was 91 feet long, 20 feet wide, and had 8.25 feet depth of hold, measuring 138 tons, all told; most important, she was driven by one of Mr. Ericsson's new screw propellors, her engine was small and was situated as far aft as it could go, and her entire hold was open for cargo. She was followed by several more vessels of the same kind, and although they were mortally slow—about five or six miles an hour was tops, and most of the time they needed their auxiliary canvas—they burned only ten cords of wood daily, which was much less than a side-wheeler of comparable size would need. Also it was noticed that, although she was small, *Vandalia* on her first trip carried 130 tons of merchandise.

At that stage of the Middle West's development, a Great Lakes steamboat was likely to make more money carrying passengers than carrying freight, and so the paddle wheel persisted on the Buffalo-Detroit-Chicago runs and on the Lake Michigan coastwise trades; if they were poorly adapted for carrying bulk freight, these side-wheelers did offer more space for passengers—the "guards," built out from the hull fore and aft of the wheel boxes, offered fine deck space and room for staterooms. Also, it took the designers a little while to see just how to make best use of the Ericsson wheel's advantages. Out of all of this, by the way, there developed an odd habit that persisted down to modern times. A steamboat—the word *ship* has never taken hold on the lakes—was a side-wheeler; a boat driven by a pro-pellor was called, quite simply and logically, a propellor.

Anyway, the propellor made possible the modern bulk carrier on the lakes, and did it just as the opening of the new canal made modern bulk carriers necessary. As they were worked out by trial and error, with everybody looking for the design that would carry the most freight at the least expense, these carriers were simply greatly overgrown canal boats, with space for engines and fuel as far aft as they would go and space for of-ficers, sailors, and navigating facilities in the extreme bow. Ev-erything in between—actually, it was a long, deep box, a great oblong cavern with a row of hatches on top—was cargo space. In sailors' lingo, it came to be said that the forward end was the captain's end of the boat, and the stern was the chief engineer's.

The advantages were overwhelming. Drawn up at the dock at Marquette or some other ore port, the boat simply removed its hatches and the ore was poured in from overhead chutes. At first, of course, the job was done by wheelbarrows and muscle power, but before long the ore dock came to be an immense crib running out into the harbor, with tracks on top, from which hop-per cars of ore could be dumped into the crib and with chutes all along the sides ready to drop the ore into the boat's hold. When the boat was fully loaded, the chutes were raised, hatches were fastened on, with tarpaulins battened down over them, and it was away for Lake Erie. Loading took a remarkably short time.

Unloading took a bit longer, but even here, the advantages were clear. The boat lay at the dock, hatches off, and various hoisting devices went to work to lift containers full of ore out and dump them in huge piles along the dock. As years passed, some of these devices grew very large and unimaginably inge-nious, and in the end it took very little longer to unload than it had taken to load; but that was for the future. Meanwhile, it turned out that it was most convenient for the unloaded ore car-riers to take coal from the Ohio ports back to Lake Superior, which had nothing to burn but hardwood and was developing huge steam-powered machines of its own. It also turned out that the bulk carriers were admirably adapted for the carriage of grain, and Chicago sent thousands of tons of wheat off to Buffalo.

So a distinctive type of carrier was evolved, for trading from the upper lakes to the ports on Lake Erie (and, later, at the foot of Lake Michigan) that received ore and grain and shipped out coal; and to this day, people in the high country, seeing the unmistakable silhouette of one of these bulk carriers, will refer to the vessel casually as "a lower-laker." It is an expression that dates a long way back, to Civil War times or thereabouts, and it probably will not endure much longer, because nothing in Michigan goes unchanged for very long. But it is a reminder of a momentous experience. With these unhandsome steamers, the United States began to knit itself into the largest consuming unit in the world. Here, for the first time anywhere, and possibly for the last time as well, a free people who were just beginning to see that they could do, physically, just about anything they could imagine themselves doing provided they had the proper materials to work with, found that their materials were in truth unlimited. (For them, and for then: with incalculable results.) Archimedes cried that, if he just had a place to stand, he could move the world. The people who built these boats and cut a channel for them and put them to work had found the place to stand. What the world would look like, after it had been moved, they had not yet found out.

8

Backwoods Production Line

$\mathcal{M}$AN'S muscles were still the primary source of power. Nothing could be done if they could not do it; they set the limits, and although for a long time they had been helped by the muscles of horses and oxen, this did not greatly change the basic rule: you can do what you are strong enough to do, and no more. So when the first assault on Michigan's pine forests was made it was exactly the kind of job King Hiram of Tyre would have understood when he set out to provide the cedar for Solomon's Temple. You took saws and axes and went to work.

Cutting the trees down and dividing them into logs was just the first step. The big thing was to turn the logs into boards, and in the beginning the only reliance was the whipsaw, which one historian called "plainly the most pernicious contraption that ever plagued a working man." [1] They began by digging a pit, six or seven feet deep, and rigging a set of cross-timbers over the top. Then a man got down into the pit with one end of a long rip saw in his hands, a log was snaked out on top of the cross timbers, and another man got on the log and laid hands on the upper end of the rip saw. After exchanging signals the two men began to work the saw up and down, up and down, and as it bit into the log still other men edged the log forward. It was slow work, and hard, and the man in the pit got the worst of it

---

1. McKee, *Great Lakes Country,* p. 187.

because the sawdust came down into his hair, his eyes, and his mouth, and stuck to his sweaty skin, and to produce a wagon-load of planks took time, strong arms and backs, and the ability to put up with abominable working conditions.

The first lumber from the Michigan pineries was cut up in this manner, and there did not seem to be much future in it. The part of the country that bought timber in quantity was the east, which was handy to the Maine forests; and Maine's pine woods, like all pine woods everywhere, were known to be inexhaustible. Still, the country was growing, and, as it grew, it needed more lumber to build houses, and the great weight of the pineries in Michigan made its pressure felt just as the weight of the metals in the north country did.

The pressure was most obvious in the Saginaw Valley. The Saginaw is deep and broad, but as an independent river it is short. It is formed by the union of five rivers—the Cass, the Flint, the Shiawassee, the Bad, and the Tittabawassee—and the last named has such tributaries as the Pine and Chippewa and Tobacco. All in all, these rivers drain a huge plat of land in the heart of the state's lower peninsula, covering half of the thumb on the east and reaching more than halfway to Lake Michigan on the west, and some of the noblest stands of pine in the new world were to be found here. If men were going to make money selling pine lumber, the Saginaw Valley was the obvious place to begin. The hand-operated pit saw might be good enough to provide boards for the local house-builders, but something better was needed if lumbermen hoped to sell on a national market.

Water-power provided part of the answer, just at first. The whipsaw was put into an oblong frame and was hitched up to a water wheel so that, as the wheel revolved, the frame moved up and down; the contraption was shaped like a window sash, and slid up and down the way a window sash does, and naturally it was referred to as a "sash saw," or sometimes as a "gate saw." It did the job all right, and it at least got the unlucky sawyer out of the pit, but it was not quite the device needed for volume production.

The first big step was taken by a man named Harvey Williams, who came up to Saginaw in 1834 and started a steam sawmill. His power plant had a history of its own. The engine came from little *Walk-in-the-Water,* first steamboat above Niagara Falls. Operating between Buffalo and Detroit, early in the 1820s, *Walk-in-the-Water* ran aground in the eastern end of Lake Erie and was wrecked. Her engine was removed and put in another boat—one of the interesting things about early Great Lakes steamboating is the way engines seemed to survive the boats that used them—and when that vessel in turn was wrecked, the engine was extracted again, and Mr. Williams bought it and took it up to Saginaw. With considerable mechanical ingenuity, he devised a rig by which the old side-wheeler engine could operate a gate saw, and the lumber industry took a step in the right direction; but the step was short, because this mill was slow and clumsy and could do little more than meet the needs of settlers in the immediate vicinity. When a new mill was built on the east side of the river, a year later, it limited itself to cutting lumber for the construction needs of the Michigan Central Railroad, and after a few years it quietly closed down.

However, the idea had been planted, and this mill was presently bought by an energetic operator named Curtis Emerson, who spent $10,000 on new machinery and found himself with a plant capable of cutting three million feet of lumber annually. (It was assumed that planks were cut one inch thick and one foot wide; such a plank, twelve feet long, would constitute twelve board feet of lumber. It was also assumed that the mill would operate on the standard twelve-hour day.) Emerson got into production, and in 1847, he shipped out the first cargo of lumber ever exported from the Saginaw Valley, sending a load of first-grade cork pine to Albany, New York.

That started it. The high quality of this lumber attracted a good deal of attention, and suddenly the market was clamoring for Saginaw pine. The firm of Grant and Hoyt built a second mill east of the river, and Sears and Holland built a third, and then things went with a rush, and in no time at all there were fourteen mills in Saginaw, with more a-building. In 1854, these turned out sixty million board feet of pine, and the lumber boom was on.

Cutting logs into boards is a task as old as civilization, but now it was geared to steam, and the old ways were no good. Once a second-hand walking-beam engine was hooked up to a gate saw, the tempo and style and the very price of survival in the industry changed beyond recognition. Do-it-by-hand was out, because mechanical power was cheaper, faster, and stronger than human power, but one rule had to be observed: it had those fine qualities only when it did as much work as possible as quickly as possible with a minimum of waste. Otherwise, it was far too costly to endure.

It was found, for instance, that a steam-powered mill making boards in quantities produced also a dismaying amount of waste material—slabs, edgings, and whole mountains of sawdust. For a time, the pioneering Emerson mill spent good money hauling this stuff away where it could be dumped; and at the same time, it spent even more good money buying cord wood to maintain the fires under its boilers. At last somebody realized that the waste woodstuffs might as well go into the furnaces, eliminating both the haulage fees and the need to buy cord wood. As business picked up, the big mills found that they produced wood-waste faster than they could use it. Some of them, toward the last, built enormous cylindrical brick consumers to burn what could not be used to power the boilers. Still others, in Saginaw and in lumber towns like Manistee, learning that valuable deposits of brine lay far underneath the mills, burned the waste to power steam pumps to bring the brine to the surface and burned more of it to evaporate the brine and produce dry salt. To the very end, however, the industry produced more slab-and-sawdust refuse than it could use, and uncounted tons of sawdust went to fill in streets and building lots; which made for an interesting situation when a building caught fire.

It was also found that the gate saw was not really efficient. The circular saw—buzz saw of popular usage—had been invented, but when it bit into a log while spinning at high speed it was apt to break its teeth; and now and then it simply flew apart and sent razor-edged fragments flying about, which was not good for the men who were running it. But at last, just as the Michigan mills were getting into production, someone invented a buzz saw with replaceable teeth held firmly in position by curved sockets, a saw that would stand up under any amount of hard usage. Also, some other operator replaced the gate saw with the gang saw, a prodigious extension of the original, which held a dozen or more vertical saw blades in one wide gate, reducing an entire log—and sometimes two or three at once—into planks in one devastating operation. Between the buzz saw and the gang saw, planks and slabs and edgings came out faster than men could handle them, so it was necessary to devise automatic conveyors to carry the planks where they had to go and take the slabs and edgings off to the furnaces, the converters, or wherever.

The mill had to be situated on a mill pond, not merely because most of the logs were floated in by river, but because the pond offered the best way to get the logs on an automatic conveyor system. Circular saws and gang saws were put on the mills's second floor, and down into the pond on a long slant came a runway, up the middle of which traveled an endless chain spiked with stout iron points every few feet. Down by the pond, which was full of waiting logs, a man with a pike pole steered the logs to the place where this endless chain would catch them, and it carried them up and dropped them on the moving carriages that took them through the battery of saws that turned them into finished lumber. This worked so well that even when mills were built on railroad supply lines, with no logs at all coming in by river, a mill pond was dug out, and the arriving logs were dumped into it from railway sidings. In winter, unfortunately, these ponds were likely to freeze, so people learned to run a few steam pipes into them, below the surface, and in January and February the ponds were kept free of ice and the logs floated off to the endless chain.

Finally, the band saw came into use— a thin band of flexible steel, notched with teeth along the edge, drawn down from one wheel by the revolution of a lower wheel, kept taut by still other wheels, slicing the pine logs up at a speed beyond even that of the circular saws. The band saw had the added advantage of being thinner than the buzz saw; it cut with a smaller kerf, as men said, which meant that much less of the log was wasted in the form of sawdust. It could square up a really big log the way a buzz saw could hardly do, and it won a place in the battery of every well-equipped mill.

The sawmill, of course, was the end of the line. The operation began in the deep woods, and originally it was gang labor, pure and simple. Also, it began as a very small-scale affair. One of the first men to cut pines on the Cass River had a gang consisting of fifteen men; they built one log shanty where everybody ate and slept, and a little room was walled off at one end for the boss man's wife, who came along to cook for the crowd.

In the early days, lumber camps averaged just about that size, and it was not uncommon for a man to recruit a logging crew and take the men to the woods before he had even lined up a stand of timber to cut. Sometimes, venturing into regions where there was nothing resembling a road by which supplies could be hauled into camp, the logger simply loaded men and their food and equipment on a scow and poled the thing up the river.

Early lumber camps were primitive, not to say repellent. One log shanty housed everybody except the oxen, which had a shanty-stable of their own. The men's shanty had no floor but packed earth, and it had no windows. There was no stove—just an open hearth of stones in the middle of the room, with a hole in the roof above to carry off the smoke. The fire that burned on this hearth cooked what the men ate and provided warmth (and a choking haze of woodsmoke) for the occupants. Bunks were platforms made of poles, with pine boughs, or sometimes hay, for mattress. Food consisted mostly of salt beef, salt pork, beans, bread, and tea, and the one certainty was that the tea was going to be strong; one old-timer remarked that it was powerful enough to raise a blister on a boot. (A very old gag: lumber-camp tea was tested by dropping an axe head into it. If the axe head sank, the tea was no good; if it floated, the tea was acceptable—and if it actually dissolved, the tea was super.) The men used to remark that the oxen were housed better than they were, and this probably was true; at least the oxen had plenty of clean straw to sleep on.

This state of things did not last long. Business expanded rapidly and the operators had to compete for men, and to get them they had to provide better food and housing. Before long, a camp had one building for a bunk house and another for cooking and eating quarters, with a stable for the animals, a blacksmith shack, and a separate building for supplies. The buildings had proper floors, and stoves with chimneys replaced the old open fireplaces; there still was next to nothing in the way of ventilation in the bunk house, although sometimes a barrel open at both ends was let into the roof. Since the men spent more than half of each twenty-four hours in the open, it was felt that they did not really need fresh air at night. The most notable improvement was in the food. Pork and beans hung on, but there were many supplements; pancakes with molasses, great platters of fried or boiled potatoes, beef stew of great staying power, canned tomatoes, pies and doughnuts and cookies without end, fresh bread and, if not actual butter, at least plenty of margarine, which the loggers unemotionally referred to as axle grease. There was always fried salt pork on the table, and slabs of corned beef, and the cook usually brewed a pork gravy that many of the men used on pancakes in place of molasses. All in all, the diet was robust and ample, and a man could do a day's work on it.

That was as well, because a day's work was certainly required of him. Six days a week, all winter and into the spring, the logger went out to work before daylight and stayed out until dark. He was aroused in the morning by the reverberating cry, "Daylight in the swamp!" This meant that he must be up, cutting down trees, so that daylight could be admitted to the swamp; contradictorily, it also meant that there was already daylight in the swamp and that therefore it was high time to be up and doing. Either way, the logger got up, pulled on his boots and mackinaw, washed his face in a tin basin, ate as much breakfast as he could hold, and headed for the tall timber. There his job was simple, but tough.

The routine was obvious: cut the tree down, remove its useless top and branches, cut the tree into logs—sixteen feet was taken as the proper length, but there was no hard-and-fast rule—and get the logs stacked up on the bank of some river down which, come spring, they could be floated to the sawmill. In the early days, a tree-length log, anywhere from seventy-five to one hundred feet long once the top had been taken off, would be dragged to the banking ground, where it was cut into logs. Hauling it there was slow work. Three or four yoke of oxen could pull almost anything, but they did not move fast, and it took a long time to get one end of this king-sized log off the ground on to a sleigh or a wishbone-shaped tree crotch known as the go-devil. Before many years, this system was largely abandoned, and the tree was cut into logs where it fell.

Axe men were the aristocrats of this sort of work, and State of Maine men were much in demand, because they had been cutting down pine trees all their lives. They worked in two-man crews, swinging their double-bitted axes in alternating blows, from right and from left, and a veteran team used to brag that if you drove a stake partway into the ground sixty feet away, they could fall a tree with such finesse that it would drive the stake in the rest of the way. (In pine woods language, by the way, the loggers would *fall* a tree, not *fell* it.) Once the tree was down, less prestigious axe men got at it and trimmed off its branches and its top, after which men with long cross-cut saws came up to reduce it to logs.

The hard work was by no means over then, because the logs still had to be taken to the banking ground by the river. Two things were necessary, above all: a roadway of sorts, and a good deal of snow and cold weather. The logs could be skidded over to the roadside by oxen or horses, using the go-devil or a device like an over-grown set of ice tongs, but at the roadside they had to be loaded on a sleigh, and since the load was usually piled up as high as a two-story house, this involved a great deal of sweating and straining. Logs are heavy, awkward to handle, and possessed of the inherent cantankerousness that sometimes gets into inanimate objects, and although horses or oxen could be used to pull on the chains that dragged the logs up on the pile, men still had to handle the logs, guiding and controlling them, adjusting their position, turning them this way and that so that the load was compact and balanced, and they could not possibly do this with their bare hands.

Originally, they used a stout pole with a ring around it and an iron hook dangling from the ring, known as a cant dog, but it was dangerously unreliable, because the hook was likely to slip sideways just as a man was putting his weight on it, and when that happened, the man could get killed. Fortunately, just about the time the Michigan boom was beginning, a blacksmith in Maine invented a new tool: strong staff of ash or rock maple, shod with iron at the lower end, with a hook swinging from a fixed hinge that kept it from slipping sideways. With this, a man could grip a log firmly, the long staff gave him the leverage he needed, and the thing would not betray him when he was handling a big log that was trying to mash him. To use it took skill—a man had to know just what he was doing on any job in the woods—but this tool was indispensable. It was known as a cant-hook. Fitted with a spike at the lower end, it was a *peavey,* named for the blacksmith who invented it; either way, they had to have it to get out the logs.

A load of logs properly stacked weighed many tons, and no wagon ever built could have carried it over a dirt road. On a sleigh it could be moved easily, always provided that the road was icy. The camp boss sent a sprinkler out at night to spray water that froze instantly, and as long as he had cold weather, all was well. Horses with calked shoes could pull on such a roadway, and if the road had no hills, there was no special problem. It was impossible to take one of these big loads up a real hill, and although going down was possible, it was extremely dangerous: if the sleigh once picked up speed, it ran over the horses, wrecked itself, and probably killed the driver. On the down-hill slopes, they scattered sand, sawdust, horse manure, ashes, whatever was handy, to reduce the danger, and a good teamster was highly prized.

In all of this, the emphasis was on speedier movement. The peavey and cant-hook set a faster tempo, the great horse-drawn sleighs moved logs to the river faster than the old method, especially when trouble was taken to keep the skid-road iced, and now someone discovered that the trees came down more quickly if cross-cut saws were used. Axe men still began by cutting a deep notch on the side where the tree was supposed to fall; but once the notch was cut they went to the opposite side and started pulling the seven-foot saw back and forth, back and forth, until at last the top of the tree swayed a bit, there was a cracking noise just where the notch had been cut, the sawyers pulled their saw out, stepped back and set up the long warning cry—"Timmmberrrr!"—and everyone near looked up and took cover. When a giant pine came down, it came down hard, and people gave it plenty of room.

One way or another, they got the logs to the banking ground. When warm weather came and the ice went out, and melting snow raised the river level, they could get the logs down to the mills; and in some ways, this was the hardest, chanciest part of the whole business.

The rivermen who took the logs down were picked crews, the best of the winter-time loggers—whose jobs, of course, were gone, once the snow melted and the roads could no longer be iced. It was up to the rivermen, first, to tumble the logs down the banks and into the water—hard enough, and often most dangerous, because the logs were piled up high on a down-hill slope, and as likely as not they would roll down with a thunderous rush, once the first two or three logs at the bottom were yanked loose. The yanking, of course, was done by rivermen with peavies, who worked with thousands of tons of logs banked up over them and who had to start running at the right second and run fast, once they got things loose.

When the logs hit the water, the real work began. In the Saginaw Valley, counting the main river and its chief tributaries, there were some 864 miles of water on which logs could be floated, draining millions of acres of woodland with an estimated 5,000 feet of timber on each acre. This of course was only one of the big river systems that came out of the pine timber lands, but it was the first to be exploited thoroughly, and it can stand as an example. The end of the line was the long chain of sawmills that lined the river banks from Saginaw to Bay City; and between the banking grounds and the mills, the rivermen marshalled a vast moving carpet of logs and tried to keep it from getting stalled anywhere. Many things could stall it—a stretch of shallow water where a few logs would run aground and pile up other logs behind them; a dry spring that lowered water levels all along the stream; a sudden freshet that sent logs drifting off into swamps and cut-over meadows and then stranded them there when the flood receded. On tributaries where the water was not deep, the rivermen built temporary dams, so that the tide of logs would move up to the dam in a great mass, and then the dam would be blown up—or, if it was a little more elaborate, a flood gate in the center would be opened—and the rush of released water would carry the logs on downstream.

Any of these things could create a log jam, which inevitably caused delay and very often killed men. A jam was a chaos of logs matted together every which way, like jackstraws, so thick sometimes that the river itself was dammed and its flow below the jam was reduced to a trickle. It was up to the rivermen to break up the jam, working along the downstream face of the mass, pecking and tugging at what looked like the key logs, opening the thing up by hook or by crook, usually getting back to the bank in time, but sometimes failing and getting mashed. Getting a log drive all the way down the river often took weeks, and the men camped out on the banks as they worked, or slept in crude floating shanties that followed the drive. The cook shack, known as the wanigan, was built on a scow, and the cook was a busy man: rivermen ate four meals a day, and sometimes five. The rivermen spent a good part of the day working thigh-deep in cold water, and when they went to bed, they were almost always more or less wet. They scorned to change to dry clothing during the drive; they believed that this caused a man to take cold and led to pneumonia, and besides they had a tough-guy tradition to live up to. As a matter of fact, they seem to have been all but indestructible.

When only one company was using a river, the operation was clear enough; but when the river was full of logs put there by eight or ten different operators, things got complicated, because all of the logs looked exactly alike. The loggers met the problem just as western cattlemen met the problem raised by a common range: they branded their stock. Before the logs went into the water, an official went along the spillway with a marking hammer and pounded the owner's brand, duly registered with the authorities, into the end of each log. Thus, when the logs got to the mouth of the stream, where the mills were, it was possible to make sure that a man's logs went to the proper consumer. On all of the major logging streams, booming companies were formed, and their employees guided the logs into big pens for delivery to the firms that had bought them.

The logging camps always closed down when warm weather came, and the hands were paid off. A few would be hired as rivermen, but most of the men simply headed for town, their pay checks in their pockets; they had worked hard all winter, living in squalid quarters and toiling under firm discipline, and now they wanted to relax, and since each man had from four to six months' pay, the lumber towns were happy to offer facilities for relaxation. A whole literature has developed about the enormous binges that rocked the foundations of these towns, and most of it is quite true; yet it is possible to suspect that there has been a great deal of exaggeration.

The same kind of over-dressing is found in the traditional accounts of life in western cow towns, where cowboys apparently spent all of their waking hours drinking whiskey, playing faro, and shooting out the overhead lights, although the cowboy, obviously, spent most of his time on the ranch or on the range and came to town to tie one on only on rare occasions. The same thing was true of the logger. He came in for a spree once a year, and that was it. No matter how freely he squandered his pay, it would last just so long, and then he was finished. About the time the loggers completed their annual orgy, the rivermen came in, all loaded for bear, but they operated under the same restraints. This was a once-a-year bender, and the wild, shouting, fighting carnival of tradition burned itself out rather quickly. The Catacombs of Bay City, the Sawdust Flats of Muskegon, and the oddly named tangles of saloons and brothels of all the other lumber towns had to subsist most of the year on the trade of regular residents. The average lumber town, to be sure, was well able to support such establishments unaided, and most of them took an inverted pride in the reputation thus gained: this year Such-and-Such was the wickedest town in Michigan, three years later it was some other place, after that it was still another, and so on, but the point is that neither the logger nor the riverman really spent much of his time drinking and roistering about. Actually, after the first years of the lumber boom, a great many of the loggers had farms in the cut-over lands, and when they got paid off, they headed for home to put in a crop, spending perhaps one evening on the town first. Others took jobs in the sawmills, which operated all summer long. A few hung around the saloons and went on the bum until autumn opened new jobs in the woods, but they burned themselves out rapidly and were never characteristic of the great mass of the lumber country's workers.

What was characteristic was that they were strong men who worked very hard with substantial skills in a calling that was always demanding and often most dangerous. They were ruthlessly exploited, from beginning to end. Pay was moderate, they had to shift for themselves more than half of each year, and if a man was hurt—as a great many were—he had to look out for his own hospitalization. As the industry grew mature, hospitals in most of the bigger lumber centers organized a hospital insurance plan, by which the logger who bought a ticket could get as much as a year's hospitalization; but it was the logger who had to buy the ticket, and if he did not have one and was sent to a hospital penniless after some accident, he wound up in the county poorhouse.

Isolated in the deep woods from November to April, the lumbermen had to provide their own amusement. Sunday was the day off, and a good part of the day was spent washing clothing and trying, usually in vain, to rid the bunks of bedbugs. Sunday evening was a time for entertainment; if there was a fiddler in camp, he had to perform, anyone who knew a song had to sing it, and poetry was recited on a dealer's-choice basis. One favorite ballad dealt with the fabulous Silver Jack Driscoll, famous as one of the toughest rough-and-tumble fighters in the woods; famous also as a man who got into so much trouble on his visits to town that he had spent several years in the state's prison. According to this poem, Silver Jack took offense one day when one Bob, a camp-mate, lounging in the bunk shanty on a Sunday afternoon, announced that he was an atheist and declared the whole Bible story a myth, adding that there was no such

place as hell. Silver Jack challenged him for this, and the two
had an epic fight, leading to a great climax:

> But at last Jack got him under
> And he slugged him onct or twice,
> And Bob straightway acknowledged
> The divinity of Christ.

After Bob had also confessed that there probably was a hell,
Silver Jack let him up. Some brought out a bottle, and the two
gladiators had a drink, and it was agreed that the fight had been
a great step forward toward righteousness:

> And we drank to Jack's religion
> In a kindly sort of way,
> And the spread of infidelity
> Was checked in camp that day.[2]

One fireside diversion was a little more rugged. One lumber-
jack would bend over, the seat of his trousers drawn tight, a
semicircle of his friends around him; one of them would give
him a hearty spank in the proper place—a blow that would
knock out an ox, as likely as not—and the victim would wheel
around and point to the man he considered responsible. If he
picked the right man, that one took his place for the next round;
if he failed, he bent over again, took another, and again tried to
identify the spanker. Somehow, this game never quite caught on
anywhere but in the lumberman's shanty. It was known, logically, as hot-ass.

In the early days, most lumber camps were small, and most
operators were working on a shoe-string basis. Right to the end,
the little fellow held a place in the industry, but the whole set-
up was obviously made for the man with ample credit and
plenty of capital, and more and more the industry was dominated by substantial capitalists. It was strictly a cyclical operation, with money going out every month of the year and coming
in just once, and there were many unpredictable things that
could cause loss. From September to November, the operator

2. Fuller, *Historic Michigan,* II:566–567.

had his gang laying out a tote-road—a rough trail leading from town to camp, so that supplies could be brought in—and building the camp itself. Late in November, he brought his gang to the camp, and from then until spring took the ice and snow off the land, everybody was at work making logs out of trees. The spring months were spent getting the logs to the mills, and it was at this time that the operator got paid. In the summer months, he was likely to be cutting marsh hay and recruiting his teams for the coming year's work.

Opportunities for going bankrupt were numerous. A mild winter was the worst thing that could happen; without snow and ice, the skid-road from cutting ground to banking ground simply could not be used, and the camp could not do much; the men might indeed cut down trees and turn them into logs, but logs that had to lie in the woods all spring and summer and fall brought in no money and could easily deteriorate. A dry spring, or a spring following a winter that was cold enough but had little snow, might mean that the river did not have enough water to float the logs away properly. Thus, in 1864, only 71 percent of the logs cut during the winter reached the market; conversely, after the fine winter of 1879, when there was plenty of snow and ice for the lumber camp crews and plenty of runoff water in the streams, the receipt of logs at the mills rose sharply—on the Menominee by more than 12 percent, on the Muskegon by 26 percent.

All of this favored the big operator and handicapped the little one. The big one could usually command enough capital to carry him through a bad year; he would not enjoy life, but at least he would survive. The little man was likely to go entirely out of business. Lumber prices had a way of fluctuating sharply from year to year, and here again the man working on a shoe-string was apt to find himself in trouble.

And yet, with all of these ways of stacking the cards in favor of the wealthy, this business did offer an opportunity to the man who was eternally industrious, canny, and now and then a bit lucky. Typically, there is the case of a 250-pound immigrant from Luxembourg, Bill Bonifas, who got to the Escanaba area in the early days and hired out doing piece-work for a contractor who was cutting cedar ties in a Garden Peninsula swamp for a railroad. Bonifas cut and carried out the six-foot cedar logs for starvation pay, but he cut and carried two logs to the other men's one, and at last he saved enough money to buy a cheap horse to haul the stuff down to the dock. When the horse proved a weakling, Bonifas got into harness with him and helped him pull. He saved more money, brought his brothers and sisters over from the old country, and at last set up a camp of his own, with his sisters doing the cooking. In the best Horatio Alger fashion, it all worked out; from cutting cedar ties, he branched out into big timber, bought pine lands, sent logs to the mills— and, not to labor the point unduly, became exceedingly wealthy and died a Grade-A lumber baron. It could be done . . . once in a while.

For with all its handicaps, the lumber industry in Michigan was basically an industry that grew great in a time when it could hardly do anything else. The great years of this industry, roughly from the early 1840s to about 1910, were years of rising emigration from Europe, and they also were years when the great rich territory from the Alleghenies to the Missouri River was filling up with towns and farms. These people needed farm houses, barns, town dwellings, stores, warehouses, sheds, and fences, and to build them they had to have immense quantities of cheap lumber. The weight of their demand was shown in one simple fact: the great wholesale center for finished lumber, which had been Albany for generations, was Chicago, after 1856. The Saginaw River, facing to the east, was developed at amazing speed, but so was the Lake Michigan trade that faced west and south, and the Muskegon became the country's great lumber river. Muskegon and Manistee, Menominee and Escanaba and Manistique, and a vast number of smaller places in between and beyond these, became indescribably busy with a great fleet of schooners carrying boards, laths, shingles, and beams down to the Chicago docks and yards. While all of this was going on, the middle-western railroads were expanding rapidly, needing timber for bridges and trestles and loading docks, sheathing for stations and cars, and incredible numbers of ties. An individual operator could of course fail if his luck ran badly, but the industry as a whole simply could not lose.

So the pressure on the industry was unceasing. King Hiram was forever out of date, and mill towns were becoming mechanized islands in an all-embracing wilderness. Sawmills, less than a generation away from the hand-operated pit saw, began to look like factories that Eli Whitney or Samuel Colt would have understood, and they attracted men who knew machinery and taught other men what machinery could do. Flint, which began strictly as a sawmill town, found itself with factories making buggies and carriages. Pontiac, another lumber town, built factories to make wagons, and developed foundries to serve its industrial plants. Grand Rapids, isolated above the rapids in the Grand River, presently was operating the world's greatest furniture factories. There were shipyards at Bay City, Port Huron, and Grand Haven, and railroad passenger cars were being built at Saginaw. These beginnings were slow and many of them came late, and none of these cities had yet freed itself from reliance on the abundance of cheap lumber. But the climate in which industrialization could take place had been created, and it was beginning to have effects.

In addition to all of this, there were the railroads, which touched the lumber industry like a bucket of turpentine tossed on a fire. Sign of their coming was the appearance of thriving lumber towns that had virtually no proper logging streams to rely on—places like Clare, Farwell, and Cadillac. It was the railroads that finally enabled the major lumber operators to escape from the primitive conditions that compelled them to idleness for half of each year. Now they were able to go on a fulltime basis.

This did not happen all at once, of course; yet the process really was not long-drawn-out. It began when people noticed that the Michigan Central and Lake Shore railroads, privately owned and completed to Chicago, were making excellent profits; it was also noticed that these railroads brought better times to the regions they served and left regions not served to struggle along as best they could. For a brief example: farmers in the western part of the state's bottom tier of counties raised much wheat, which was their only cash crop; they had trouble getting it to the port of St. Joseph, where boats could take it to the Chicago market. To avoid a ruinously expensive wagon haul, farmers living near the St. Joseph River built what they called "arks"— big square boxes of cheap lumber, some of them forty feet long, resembling boats only in that they would float. These were piled full of wheat and with a man or two to guide them (and very little guidance was possible, aside from fending them off the shallow places with long poles), they were floated down to the docks at St. Joseph. The arks were so little regarded that they were either sold for what their lumber would bring, which was next to nothing, or were simply abandoned and allowed to drift wherever they chose, out on Lake Michigan. The new railroad relieved the farmers of this burden, no more arks were made, and the cash position of the man who raised wheat improved.

So the pressure for more railroads became strong, and results were soon evident. At Toledo, the Lake Shore already hooked up with a line to Cleveland, the Michigan Central made connections with Buffalo via Ontario's Great Western Railroad; and in the early 1850s, Buffalo had a regular railroad route to Albany and thence to New York. Of more immediate importance to the lumber man in Michigan was the fact that, before the Civil War, a line was pushed through from Detroit, by way of Pontiac and Grand Rapids, to Grand Haven, on the Lake Michigan shore. At the same time, the general enthusiasm for railroads induced Congress to make lavish grants of public land to subsidize railroad construction, and Michigan was awarded more than 3,800,000 acres, which the state authorities promptly augmented by making an additional grant of more than 1,500,000 acres. After some spirited in-fighting among various interested parties—with a pie of this size being cut, everybody came running to the table—a number of routes were blocked out, and construction was started. There was inevitably much delay, waste, and lost motion, but the upper peninsula got lines tying Marquette in with both Escanaba and Ontonagon; and in addition to lower peninsula lines aimed at the Straits, there was a road that connected Port Huron, Flint, and Saginaw with the booming lumber town of Ludington, at the mouth of the Pere Marquette River on Lake Michigan. This road was in full operation by 1874, and the first step away from half-time lumbering was taken.

For it quickly became obvious that a logger need not be compelled to get his logs to a river and that a sawmill town did not need to be situated at the river's mouth. If the lumber camp was on a railroad, the logs could come out, regardless of the rivers; and if the milltown was on a railroad, it could get the logs and ship out the boards. Water transportation was still cheaper, but it was no longer an essential.

The next step was not long delayed. In 1876, a young lumberman named Scott Gerish, who owned a fine stand of pine in Clare County, just a little too far away from the Muskegon River, visited the Centennial Exposition in Philadelphia and saw a narrow-gauge locomotive on display. The engine was light and cheap, so were the cars it would pull, and so also was the track it would run on, and a great light dawned on Mr. Gerish. A narrow-gauge railroad could be a temporary thing; you could run it through the woods without worrying about what the right-of-way would be like fifty years later, because, fifty years later, you would be long gone. The whole business was cheap, light, adaptable, and expendable. Mr. Gerish formed a small stock company and ran a narrow-gauge line from the heart of the deep woods to a convenient spot on the Muskegon River. The winter was mild, with hardly any snow and very little ice, and boss loggers either went broke or pulled in their belts and waited stoically for next year; Mr. Gerish ran his railroad, got his full consignment of logs over to the river, got other logs out, at a price, for other loggers in that area, and made a most handsome profit.

The point was too obvious to miss. Gerish's tract of pines was about ten miles from the river: unreachable, according to old standards, unless he could build dams to flood some insignificant creeks and got blessed with a cold and blizzardy winter. With his pint-sized railroad, which could be picked up and taken somewhere else after it had done its work, he could get his logs to market easily and cheaply while other men were going bankrupt. All at once, the vast stands of pine that had been written off because they were a few miles too far from running water became immediately available. Inside of six years, there were forty-nine of these little railroads in operation in central Michigan, and lumber was going to the market so rapidly that the price began to fall.

One thing led to another. Once it was clear that logs could be got out, regardless of the state of the winter weather, men tackled the problem of getting logs from the place where the trees were cut down to the place where the logs would be loaded. Some bright man in Manistee devised the Big Wheels: a pair of monstrous wheels, ten or twelve feet in diameter, with a wagon tongue hooked up with hoisting leverage. Three or four logs could be straddled by this big go-cart, front ends lifted off the ground, and an ox team or a pair of Percherons could haul the load from falling ground to railroad siding, at which point, by somebody else's ingenuity, there was a donkey engine and a derrick to pick the logs up and stack them on the flat cars. It became possible to make logging a year-round proposition. R. G. Peters of Manistee devised a high-wire conveyor system, cutting off the tops of tall trees, running taut cables from one to the next, skidding tongs on wheels dangling beneath, picking up logs and whisking them cross-lots to wherever they were supposed to go. Mr. Peters came in just a bit late with this idea, but it grew great in the far west when the tall timber there came in for destruction.

The point of all of this is that lumbering ceased to be a winter-time occupation. The logging streams of course were used right to the last, but by the final twenty years of the century the industry no longer depended on them, nor did it depend on the ice and snow a cold winter would bring. From the whispering pine trees in the remotest grove down to the lumber dealer's yard in Chicago or Omaha, lumber was on a production line. Machine-shop efficiency had come to the wilderness, everybody prospered, and there was only one trouble. Just as they got everything perfected they ran out of trees.

9

Members of the Community

$\mathcal{B}$Y the middle of the nineteenth century, Michigan's development was carrying the state to contradictory extremes. It was becoming the home of an individualism so intense that each man seemed to be pitted against all other men, and the land-looker's desperate race to the land office might stand for every man's condition. Yet, at the same time, these individualists who pursued unlimited opportunity with unlimited desires knew that they owed their very existence to a profound unity with other men whom they never saw but whom they could not possibly ignore.

French Alexis de Tocqueville, commenting on individualism run riot in the new world, might have been speaking for the people of this state who killed animals, destroyed forests, and gouged metal out of the eternal hills with no thought of restraint: "They owe nothing to any man, they expect nothing from any man; they acquire the habit of always considering themselves as standing alone, and they are apt to imagine that their whole destiny is in their own hands." [1]

It only seemed that way. This state had never been a colony; it had been created by the central government, it was the central government that financed the life-giving canals and railroads,

1. Alexis de Tocquevillè, *Democracy in America,* translated by Henry Reeve, 2 vols. (New York: G. Dearborn & Company, Etc., 1838), II:106.

and it was the rising demand of the people of a constantly growing nation that brought profit to mines, sawmills, and wheat
fields. When the Civil War broke out, there was never the least
question how this state would line up. Early in February 1861,
the legislature contemptuously refused to send delegates to the
abortive peace conference that vainly tried to work out a compromise; it resolved that the secessionist states were "in open
rebellion against the government" and pledged all of the state's
men and money to the government's support, saying that "con-
cession and compromise are not to be entertained, or offered to
traitors." [2] When the fighting began, it supported these bold
words with vigor; Michigan sent 87,000 men into federal service, and 14,700 of them lost their lives.

Yet if people believed instinctively in a unity that they were
willing to defend to the death, the appeal of this noble vision
never made them lose sight of the main chance. Giving much,
they also demanded much. They had to, as a matter of fact,
because the help they required had to come before anyone could
gain anything. The great canal at the Soo had to be built before
the traffic that would justify it even existed, and the railroads
built with those lavish land grants must be laid out and nailed
down before there was anyone to ride on them or send goods by
them. This was even the case with the Great Lakes themselves,
which seemed to have been created by a thoughtful Providence
in order to carry the heavy commerce of a mighty people. These
lakes were broad and deep but they needed a great deal of extensive remodeling before they could serve that purpose, and
that remodeling must be approved and financed by a distant
Congress which, when it looked west, could see no more than
an insignificant trickle of small boats carrying nothing much.

All of this reversed the usual process. Ordinarily, you spent
money on transportation lines to serve a pressing need; here, it
was necessary to create the need in order to serve it after the
money had been spent. You took things on faith, and the New
Testament notion that faith can move mountains was powerfully
endorsed on the shores of the two peninsulas. It was believed

2. Bruce Catton, *The Coming Fury* (New York: Doubleday, 1961), p. 268.

that people would infallibly do what they *could* do; the idea that they certainly could do whatever they wanted to do came a little later, but it came, inevitably; and, all in all, it was about the most unsettling idea the human race ever got.

Meanwhile, there was the day's work to do, and the men who took sidewheelers or schooners up from Chicago, through the straits, and down by Detroit to Lake Erie, had problems. Lakes Michigan and Huron run north and south, and the prevailing winds in the Middle West—which can be almighty strong, on occasion—blow from the west. The biggest trouble a skipper had was that he was never far from a lee shore and that there was no harbor of refuge. He could not heave to and drift before the wind, as he could do on the open ocean, because, if he did, he would be on the beach, or on an offshore reef or sand bar, in no time at all. He simply had no place to go when a storm came up. Muskegon lay on a sheltered lake that communicated with Lake Michigan, and if a sailor could make it through the shallow opening, he was all right; and Grand Traverse Bay, farther north, offered a haven, although, in the early days there, the haven had no town, no shipyard, no stores, and no help of any kind for a battered craft that came in to get out of the storm. Aside from these places there were rivers and creeks with sandbars cutting them off from the big lake, and although it was obvious that these would offer good harbors, if somebody dredged out the openings, there was nobody nearer than Washington with the money and ability to do the dredging.

Michigan, Wisconsin, and Illinois called frantically for help from Washington, but senators and congressmen who looked west saw uninhabited shores flanking a broad waterway that was not used by anybody in particular, and so they did very little. A merchant in Milwaukee in 1840 wrote indignantly: "The steamboat *Champlain*, the brig *Queen Charlotte*, and four or five schooners, are ashore, and some of them total wrecks, and what a pity it is that they were not all loaded with senators and members of Congress." [3] The senators and representatives

3. Thomas L. Odle, "The Commercial Issues of the Great Lakes and the Campaign Issues of 1860," in *Michigan History*, XL, no. 1:5*ff*.

avoided shipwreck, but at last they got the idea, and the shores of the lakes got public works, dredging and heavy stone breakwaters and lighthouses and life-saving stations in profusion, and finally everything was in order.

The point is that the highways in this robust land had to generate their own traffic. Railroads and waterways came into being because men believed they would be used. Everybody seemed to be engaged in a huge gamble, and in a curious inversion of the well-known theological principle, they expected good works to be justified by faith. At a time when occupation of the upper half of the lower peninsula was limited to river-mouth sawmill towns and fishing outposts on Lake Huron and Lake Michigan, two railroad lines were being pushed northward to connect lonely, unimportant Mackinaw City with the thriving, populous belt that ran west from the Detroit River and the southern end of Saginaw Bay. These railroads were bridges to the future; they plunged deeply into the untouched pine forests, throwing out lumbermen as flankers and skirmishers as they advanced, and the high-pitched whine of the buzz saws was heard in places that had never known a sound louder than the self-betraying whisper of the upper branches of the pines. Before long, there were three main north-south lines, one of them running up from Chicago and Grand Rapids to the Little Traverse Bay country and the other two going to the Straits, one touching the Lake Huron shore at Alpena and the other following a more central route and touching no town that had even existed before the track gangs came along.

The men who built these roads were not notable as visionaries who took things on faith. They knew exactly where they were going and what they were doing, led on by the knowledge that a great many logs were going to be moved in the immediate future and by the even more comforting awareness that the great land-grants invited them to play a game in which it was almost impossible for them to lose. Under the standard terms, a building railroad got alternate sections of land for a distance of six miles on each side of the right of way; to put it more clearly, it was given half of all the acreage in a belt of land twelve miles wide. The railroad builders had had their own land-lookers out and, with a little care, they could build into the best pine lands. They also enjoyed close relations with speculators who had bought up other good lands—buying, sometimes, with the canniness born of inside knowledge about where the railroad was going to go—and all in all, it appears that some of these vigorous entrepreneurs were dealing themselves cards from a thoroughly stacked deck. Much of the time it paid to build a railroad even without taking into consideration the money the completed railroad was going to earn.

Yet, somehow, looking back, the fact that a few thoughtful men got rich at the public expense does not seem especially important. What really mattered was that the state was wholly transformed in an extremely short time. North of the latitude of Saginaw, it had been almost totally primitive; suddenly, the time measured in mere decades, it became an integral unit in modern industrial society. Characteristically, it was fated to abandon its railroads just as it got them perfected; but, while they lasted, it used them to profound effect. Nobody really planned very much of this. The land grants laid out a general idea, rather than a pattern. Blind and impersonal forces that no one controlled were at work.

The upper peninsula contained minerals that compelled the creation of a canal at the Soo; they also compelled the building of railroads, and they were at least partly responsible for the building of the two lower peninsula lines to Mackinaw City. The canal made it possible to ship iron ore and copper to the lower lakes in bulk, but railroads were needed to get these from the mines to dock-side. It quickly appeared, also, that the upper peninsula had its own rich pine forests, and these needed railroad transportation even more than the ones farther south did. Marquette had to have railroads to its iron range, copper-town Houghton needed a rail line to the south, there had to be a line to tap the Menominee Range, eventually there was needed a road running from the Soo to Marquette and Ontonagon, (and on to Duluth, finally) and there must be a branch going down to St. Ignace, where car ferries would take trains across the Straits and offer the high country direct connection with Detroit. All of this had to be done, and the land-grant system financed it, and the frozen country where mails moved once a month by snow-shoe and toboggan, and people who could not get out hibernated for the winter, discovered that it was no longer isolated. It was still a long way from anywhere, but compared to what it had been, it was right in the thick of things.

By and large, the men who built all of these railroads, whether above or below the Straits, had to look to the future, and they understood perfectly well (regardless of what local boosters and speculators might say) that the forests were not going to last forever. Sooner or later, the trees would all be gone; the railroads, both standard-gauge and narrow-gauge, made it possible now to take out the hardwoods as well as the pines; aspen saplings could go to the pulp mills, and anything that had roots and bark was going to be cut down. When that day came, the railroads would be out of business, unless some-body settled the cut-over land and made farms there. Wheat and apples and corn and livestock made revenue freight just as well as logs and boards made it, and everybody looked forward to a time when the northern part of Michigan would be just like the southern part—a happy land in which prosperous farmers cul-tivated good fields, sent crops off to market, and shared in a prosperity that they themselves had helped to create.

This obviously was a fine idea, and what the state needed most was a happy land full of red-cheeked settlers. Publicly and privately, the state undertook to get them. It would actively promote immigration, and if it had to go all the way to Europe to get it, that it would readily do.

So in January of 1881, Governor David Jerome announced that the state contained millions of acres of good farm lands, made available by the extensive building of railroads. If settlers came in to use these lands, the state would profit greatly. There-fore, "to secure our share of the emigrants now landing upon the shores of the United States," [4] Michigan would do its best to acquaint these people with the rich, numerous, and varied resources available in the state. It would set up immigration

---

4. Robert Warner and C. Warren Vanderhill, editors, *A Michigan Reader: 1865 to the Present* (Grand Rapids: William B. Eerdmans Publishing Co., 1974), pp. 62–66.

commissioners, and it trusted that railroads and traders who had land to sell would actively canvass the new arrivals to steer as many of them as possible into Michigan. This advice was heeded, especially by the railroads, some of which sent agents all the way to Europe and convinced people who did not know Michigan from Timbuctoo that fine times awaited them in the stump-land along the line of the Grand Rapids and Indiana or the Michigan Central.

This official enthusiasm soon cooled. In 1885, a new governor, Josiah W. Begole, felt that the operations of the state's immigration bureau "have been disastrous to our workingmen." Job-hunters were swarming in at a time when jobs were scarce; the labor market was "over-crowded from abroad" just at a time when "our laboring men were suffering for want of remunerative employment," [5] and the governor darkly suspected that the state's effort to attract immigrants was really a scheme to give free advertising to the efforts of the railroads to unload their surplus lands.

It may be wholly coincidental, but 1885, when Governor Begole was so gloomy, was a year when there was widespread unrest on the part of the men who worked in the sawmills. Bay City and Saginaw had serious strikes, with sawmill hands demanding that the twelve-hour day be reduced to ten hours without a reduction in pay, and there were parades by workers whose battle cry was: "Ten hours or no sawdust." The strikers had practically everything working against them, chiefly the fact that the Saginaw Valley's day as a major lumber producer was just about over; the mill owners were happy enough to reduce the work-day to ten hours, but they flatly refused to reduce the hours without also reducing the pay, and they knew very well that in a short time they were all going to have to shut up shop and go somewhere else. When one of the principal owners remarked that, if "the rule of mobs" were not curbed, "we propose to close our mill and all business there and not resume it," [6] he meant exactly what he said. The strike was broken, not

5. Warner and Vanderhill, *A Michigan Reader,* pp. 62–66.
6. Anita Shafer Goodstein, "A New York Capitalist in Michigan's Forests," in Warner and Vanderhill, *A Michigan Reader,* p. 54.

without bitterness; but obviously this was no time for elected people to try to bring more wage-earners into the state.

The picture got even darker very soon. In 1887, Governor Russell Alger found new reasons for curbing immigration. "An examination of the records of our asylums, prisons, poorhouses and jails," he declared, "will startle you when you find the great per cent of inmates that are foreign born." The immigrants brought in "bad people of all classes and conditions," criminals, paupers, lunatics, cripples, and decrepit senior citizens of all sorts, and the state's taxpayers had to support them. The country was also threatened by "a horde of Chinese Pagans," and although these had not yet begun to infest Michigan, care should be taken. Just to be sure he had not overlooked any menace, the governor added that the polygamy notoriously accompanied by Mormonism ought to be checked, and Congress should be urged to end "this blot upon our flag and disgrace to our nation." [7]

There is of course no way to check a native-bred flannel-mouth when he gets thoroughly wound up, and Governor Alger had his say; but apparently no one paid very much attention. Immigration to Michigan continued, not unaffected by the fact that, despite the horrors seen by governors, the railroads and other important people had cut-over lands to dispose of.

Besides, the state's history ran the other way. It had been needing and using immigrants ever since the War of 1812, and it would need and use ever so many more of them in the years following Governor Alger's gloomy remarks. Cornishmen were working the great mines up north, and Finns were proving excellent woodsmen whom the rigors of a Northern Michigan winter could not frighten. Swedes and Norwegians and Danes were coming in to work beside the Finns and the French Canadians in the lumber camps north and south of the Straits, and great numbers of hard-working people from Holland were developing a broad belt of farm land from Grand Rapids to Lake Michigan, founding a sober-sides town by the big lake and brightening it up with wooden-shoe festivals and great fields of tulips. Irish escaping from overseas famine were crossing Can-

ada to enter Detroit and fan out to the camps and mills and
railway lines, and colonies of Germans and Italians were going
into southern Michigan towns for jobs in shops and factories;
and all of these people together became one more of those inexhaustible resources the people of Michigan were forever talking
about, heaping confusion on the counsels of the backwards-
lookers who believed that New Jerusalem could be inhabited
only by the orthodox. Of all the states in the Union, Michigan
was just about the last in which to preach that the immigrant
was no better than a burden on the taxpayer. As a matter of fact,
the immigrant *was* the taxpayer.

So Michigan invited the immigrant, despite timorous governors, and it was led on by an entrancing vision.

In the southern part of the state, the destruction of the forests
had been followed quickly and easily by the creation of productive farms, and the cross-state railroad lines in the bottom tiers
of counties prospered mightily because of this. Just at first, it
was natural to think that the same story would be true farther
north, and now and then men who thought about the boundless
acres that were about to open before the homesteader and his
plow grew fairly lyrical. Most lyrical of all, probably, was an
editor who gazed upon the destruction of the last great forests in
the upper peninsula and found himself verging on ecstasy. He
announced that he saw a future for this land

> where as the forests gradually fade, the procession of agriculturists
> follow in the wake of the woodsman's axe and convert the wilder-
> ness of stumps into gardens of roses, into fields bountifully laden
> with grain, and pastures peopled with live stock, so that instead of
> the milk of the past in the future it will be cream, and the cream and
> honey will flow in continuous and ever-increasing volume because
> of the bounteous production of our rich and varied soils, varied as
> are the timber harvests they have produced but each in turn rich in
> the possibilities of their future harvests.[8]

Although he suffered from a complete inability to turn himself
off, this man had a fairly common vision: the state was going to

8. Alvah L. Sawyer, "The Forests of the Upper Peninsula and Their Place in History," Fuller, *Historic Michigan,* II:584.

be one big productive garden, just as soon as the last of the pine stumps had been grubbed out.

It was natural for men to feel that way. The land of cream and honey could actually be seen, touched, and lived in, down below the pineries. Get the forests out of the way, and you would get rose gardens and all the rest, and everybody would be happy, so let's get on with it—except that it at last became clear that the pine country was cursed by poor soil and too much cold weather. It did have its fertile spots. There was a narrow strip along the Lake Michigan shore that was ideal country for growing apples, cherries, and peaches, and there were pockets of tolerably good soil scattered here and there, all the way to Lake Superior; but in the main, the de-forested country was good for growing pine trees and not much good for anything else.

Railroads that thrust long lines up and down and across this land, confident that the farmer would provide pay loads long after the logger had gone elsewhere, learned this the hard way and began a process of going broke that continued until hardly any of them were left alive. Hopeful little towns that had sprung up to provide markets and trading centers began to dwindle into a dreary succession of boarded-up stores, crumbling foundation stones in weedy vacant lots, and decayed, paintless warehouses leaning against one another by side-tracks that no longer existed. Worst of all was the unending succession of abandoned farms, places whose people had put in a life-time of work and then had just given up and moved out, letting the state take over under the tax delinquency laws. Some of the farmhouses were torn down for the lumber that was in them, and others simply collapsed and disappeared, their place marked by great lilac windbreaks which put a fragrance on the air to testify that something would grow up here, even if it did not have much market value.

As all of this happened, a strange cycle began to take form. The wilderness that had been killed with such energy and wholehearted determination started to creep back. The empty land that could do nothing else grew trees again, and although not all of them would ever be worth very much at the sawmill, they at least made up forests, offering shelter for wild animals and cool shade for tired folk from the cities, and the returning wilderness was welcomed. People could hunt game and catch fish there, and build cabins and cottages by rivers and lakes that once had been lined with lumber camps and sawmills, and it began to be seen that people who could no longer bring forth anything that could be sent off to market might at least make a living by providing relaxation and recreation to businessmen and wage earners from busier places. Before the expression passed into popular usage, a great many people in Michigan learned what service industries are.

The different phases of development overlapped most confusingly. Creaky paddle-wheelers had been carrying pleasure cruisers up from the lower lakes before the fur traders had stopped portaging their bales down past the Soo rapids. Lumbermen were booming logs to the sawmills on the Saginaw while out-of-state sportsmen were still killing trophy elk on that river's upper tributaries. The railroads that finally reached the Straits found themselves, almost immediately, doing a rousing trade, carrying summer people north to the land of cool summers and clear waters, and resort hotels and summer cottages were built on the edges of forests that were being torn apart on the farther side by men with double-bitted axes and crosscut saws. Summer is a hot, steamy time in the Ohio and Mississippi valleys, and the northland had an irresistible appeal for men and women in the crowded cities.

United States regulars were still posted to the picturesque fort on Mackinac Island, even though they were not in the least needed there, and people on the verandas of the island's hotels considered that the soldiers enhanced the place's romantic appeal. Sports fishermen got into some areas ahead of the loggers themselves; and as early as 1882, one of them wrote about camping for two weeks on Crooked Lake, taking black bass at the rate (or so he said, anyway) of one catch for each cast, and he taunted his unlucky fellows farther south:

> Think of this, ye who fish for suckers and catfish in the swamp streams of Indiana and in the roily waters of the Kankakee—the experience of one who has cast his line in the sunny South, in the streams of the far West, and in our own beautiful Michigan, reads

like a very fairy tale. No flies to bother you as up in Canada—no 'skeeters nor any no-see-'ums—nothing to mar the pleasures—no hot stifling nights, no clammy dews, no dank miasma creeping into the system; but rest—sweet sleep at night and a dreamy existence by day.[9]

It is clear that the vacation-country booster had attained a lusty development very early in the game, and his tribe has not grown any weaker in the years since then. One truth at least became self-evident long ago: northern Michigan may have been a fine place for some people to make money—with luck, even to strike it rich—but it was an even better place to relax and enjoy life.

But it was not, over all too many of its acres, a good place to make a farm. It became apparent long afterward that a great many lumber-country farms were actually subsistence farms, part-time operations at best: the farmer did what he could to raise a crop from mid-spring to mid-autumn, and then went to work in the lumber camp the rest of the time, and between the two, he just managed a living for himself and his family. When the lumber camps went out of existence and his winter-time job disappeared, he learned that his farm by itself could not support him. In thousands of cases, the man and his family simply went away and let the painfully cleared acres go back to sumac and stubbly aspens. The top soil was just too thin, and after a few years it was exhausted, and there was nothing underneath it but sand and gravel.

Of course this was not universally true. There were patches of land that could be farmed, with proper care, year after year, and men who were willing to work hard often made a go of it where less determined folk gave up and headed for the cities and their factories. But this north country farming was never much like the farming in the richer lands to the south. It offered pioneering with the bark on, and the survivors seldom wrote rhapsodies about the pleasures of rural life in northern Michigan.

Even at best, it was no life for softies. When a family put up

9. J. A. Van Fleet, *Summer Resorts of the Mackinac Region* (1882; reprint ed., Grand Rapids: Black Letter Press, 1970), pp. 32–33.

a one-room cabin and cut down enough trees to provide space for a little crop, it had to settle down for a few years of (as it was known) grubbing for a living. A woman descended from pioneer settlers, compiling a history of the early days, looked into this expression to find out just what it meant. She learned that it involved taking mattocks and going out to grub up the tough roots that ran everywhere just under the surface, because, until these were removed, the land could not be plowed, and there could be no real farm. Reflecting on this, she remarked that she could see what the old expression implied: *"very* hard work!"

Up in the railroad land-grant country, things were complicated, and in addition to all of the hard work, there was an encompassing loneliness that was too much for some people to endure. The square-mile sections of forest land were laid out in a checkerboard pattern, so that each square mile of land available to settlers was surrounded on each side by a square mile whose trees would remain untouched until the railroad sold the land to some lumber company. The average settler tried to get 160 acres, a quarter section, and the square mile open to ordinary purchasers would have room for only four of them. This meant that the family that put up a shelter and started the infinitely toilsome job of turning it into a farm had only three neighbors at best, and was surrounded on all sides by the densest wilderness. There was not a great deal of sunlight around because, for the first years, all the clearings were very small; roads usually were little more than blazed trails, and if the settler had any pigs or cattle, he had to be careful lest the wolves and panthers got them. These beasts were not dangerous to human beings, but their howls and screams on winter nights emphasized the isolation. People who grubbed out a living in these circumstances needed to be individualists of the most rugged sort, but they quickly came to feel warm attachment for their neighbors. The sense of community became very strong in those clearings that flickered like hopeful campfires in the endless wilderness night.

Some people could take it, and some could not. There was a man named Benjamin Hall, who came into Wexford County in the heart of the railroad-grant country in 1862 and bought a tract of land near the Manistee River; he came in by ox-drawn wagon, with his wife and a little furniture and odds and ends of equipment, and for a few months the Halls lived in the wagon while he worked to make enough of a clearing to raise turnips, which would get the family and the livestock through the winter. He did not have time to build a regular cabin, but raised a pole-and-bark affair that apparently was neither better nor worse than the aboriginal wigwam of the Ottawas. It had a dirt floor, a fireplace of loose stones, and a section or two of tin stovepipe for a chimney, and the people who wintered in it were subsisting largely on turnips. It is not surprising to learn that, after a year or so of this, Mrs. Hall ran away and was seen no more. Hall remarried, after a time, assuming that his wife had died or had divorced him, and his second wife also ran off, after sticking it out for two years. Undaunted, or possibly just plain lonely, Hall married a third time, and this Mrs. Hall insisted that she would not stay in this wilderness farm unless he built a proper house. He did so, all was well, and by the end of his life, this vigorous pioneer had a regular farm in production. But it had taken him three wives and all of his life to do it.

For a long time, his only neighbor was a Dr. Perry, who was pioneering at the age of seventy—a man who had never gone to medical college or gained a medical degree but who did know something about medicine and was accepted on the frontier as a regular physician, partly, no doubt, because for seven years he was the only doctor there was in those parts. On the frontier, if you helped others, they helped you and took you at your own valuation.

An interesting sample case is that of Zachariah and Mary Morgan, who went up to the edge of Pine Lake in 1870 and carved out a home when no one but vanished Indians and elusive land-lookers had ever seen that part of the country. To the east, a railroad was slowly laying out a right-of-way from Grand Rapids to Little Traverse Bay; westward, where a stream from Pine Lake went out through a little pond to Lake Michigan, a fishing village kept itself alive by shipping whitefish down to Chicago and selling cordwoood to the steamers that carried it. In between the unbuilt railroad and the undeveloped village, there was nothing at all but the long reach of Pine Lake and rolling stretches of unbroken forest. The Morgans picked this country to make their home.

The Morgans were just like all the other pioneers, but it must be born in mind that they were black. Zachariah Morgan had been born in 1840, the son of manumitted slaves in North Carolina. When he was halfway through his childhood, his parents feared that kidnapers would snatch him up and sell him South— a fear Southern black folk had to live with even when they themselves were no longer in bondage—and so they took him to Canada, living there until 1860, when they moved to Haiti, which was appealing to American blacks as a haven where they could find full equality and boundless opportunity. Mary Nevitt, four years younger than Zachariah, was the daughter of fugitive slaves from Washington, and they had fled to Canada and had gone on to Haiti, just as the Morgans had done. Zachariah and Mary met in Haiti, married, had two sons, and in 1870 concluded that Haiti's attractions were illusory and returned to the United States. They had a little money, a married sister of Zachariah lived in northern Michigan, and to Michigan Zachariah and Mary made their way, going by steamer to Northport, finding there a sailboat that took them to the mouth of Pine River, and going on by rowboat to the home of the sister, Mrs. Louisa Burton. Morgan had bought land on another part of Pine Lake, and after a few days, he and two of his sister's neighbors went over to the site with axes, cut down some trees, and began to build a cabin.

From that point on, it is a typical pioneer story. The cabin went up one log at a time, all by hand—neither Morgan nor the volunteer helpers had horses or oxen—and when it was finished, the Morgans moved in, cleared away brush and leaves from the place where the cabin trees had been cut down, and got in a crop, and Morgan used his saw and axe to make beds and chairs and other furniture. The nearest store was at Charlevoix, twenty-four miles away, and Morgan tramped over there to buy flour, corn meal, lard, brown sugar, soda, and kerosene, rigging a harness to take the load on his back, and making the two-day trip back to his cabin with it.

The first years were slow going, full of hard work; one summer, Morgan went to Charlevoix and got a job to bring in a little money while the new farm was getting established, leaving his two boys, neither of whom was yet ten years old, to do the chores and look after Mrs. Morgan. During the next few years, other settlers came, and the Morgans helped them get settled just as they themselves had been helped by Mrs. Burton's neighbors; little by little they prospered, and when the railroad went through to Little Traverse Bay and a town named Boyne City was platted near the mouth of the Boyne River, Morgan had some money to invest in land there. It was Morgan who led in the organizing of the first school district in that neighborhood and who became a principal communicant in the first church that was established; it was also Morgan who set up a brickyard, and when a new four-room school was built, it was built with Morgan's bricks, and two Morgan children were in its first graduating class.

It was all typical. Morgan died in 1894, a prosperous farmer, one of the leading citizens of the town he had helped to build. His wife survived him by many years, and when the Methodist Church celebrated its diamond anniversary in 1949, she was the guest of honor, the only living charter member—an incredible 105 years old. She died two years later, survived by sixty-eight descendants, and all business places in Boyne City were closed for the funeral, businessmen were her pallbearers, city and county officials were in attendance, and people agreed that, for eighty years, she had given help and friendship to people who came in to make their homes and that she had given strength and character to the community simply because she had strength and character of her own and liked to share them. And she was exactly like all the other pioneer women in that area, except for one thing: she lived longer than anybody else did.

Now the Morgans were examples of complete individualism operating against a background of total unity. They survived and prospered by their own efforts, which were prodigious, beating the enormous racial handicap simply by acting as if it did not exist; yet, as pioneers, they got help from others, gave it in return, and helped create something that would not have come into being if many diverse people had not happily worked together. As Tocqueville remarked, they acted as if their whole destiny were in their own hands, but when they reached out to grasp it they found themselves joining hands with others. The real heroes of the story are never the self-seekers who won fame and riches; they are the individualists who are made larger than themselves by membership in the community.

10

The Inexhaustible Resource

*A*society that married the patient industry of the ant to the blithe improvidence of the grasshopper had much to learn, and it had to be its own teacher. The ultimate discovery—that a day of infinite possibilities imposes infinite responsibilities—was still in the future, but an essential first step was to accept change as part of the natural order. A governor might bleat that immigrants brought crime, disease, and pauperism in their pitiful bundles of worldly goods, but he was simply looking to the past at a moment when the future was about to overwhelm him. A collective will was beginning to find expression, and now and then perplexing incidents occurred.

There was, for instance, the case of Abel F. Fitch and the Great Railroad Conspiracy.

Fitch was full of energy and achievement. He came to Michigan from Connecticut in 1832, opened a tavern on the Territorial Road near Jackson, made a success of it, got into real estate, was in and out of a wildcat bank, and finally helped to organize the town of Michigan Center, of which he quickly became the leading citizen. He helped put together the local caucus of the Democratic party, was township supervisor and head of a cavalry squadron in the state militia, occupied a 500-acre farm near town, and at forty-three could pride himself on being a well-to-do man of unblemished reputation who could live serenely and enjoy life. Obviously, he was a go-getter who knew just where to go and what to get; and at the same time, he and the people around him were members one of another and the knowledge would not let him rest. He became the local leader in the underground railroad which, in the last twenty years before the Civil War made it obsolete, passed thousands of fugitive slaves on to Detroit, the big river, and final freedom in Canada; it also helped cultivate among the new settlers a firm antislavery sentiment that was an important factor in the days after Fort Sumter. (The state used to boast, rightly or wrongly, that the first slave freed by Union troops was one George Smith, liberated from bondage at Alexandria, Virginia, by the First Michigan Infantry in May 1861). In the 1850s, moved apparently by nothing much more than a sense of duty to his fellows and an instinctive antagonism to powerful folk who tried to shove people around, Fitch took on the Michigan Central Railroad in mortal combat.

The Michigan Central was then the dominant economic power in the state. It was one of those state-owned lines that the authorities had been glad to unload in 1846, and it had been taken over by two Detroit capitalists, John W. Brooks and James F. Joy, who enlisted some important Boston money to get the new corporation off to a good start. They bought the road on uncommonly favorable terms. State bonds were then selling at seventy cents on the dollar, but the state agreed to accept them at full par value in payment for the railroad property. It also gave the Central a monopoly on east-west railroad traffic via Detroit; no other line could build within five miles of the Central's line without Central's permission, and no railroad could build within twenty miles of Detroit if its line ran, on the average, less than twenty miles from the Central. In return, the new road had to extend its line to Chicago inside of three years and the existing line, from Detroit to Kalamazoo, had to be rebuilt; but the Chicago-Detroit traffic was obviously going to be a gold mine, and a heavier roadbed and new equipment would quickly pay for themselves. The Michigan Central got off to an extremely good start, and by 1849 its net earnings ran to $200,000 a year.

While it was thriving and prospering, the Michigan Central

got into trouble with the farmers who lived along the line. The railroad right-of-way was not fenced, and on its way through broad pasture land, it was operated by men firm in the faith that railroad tracks were for trains and not for livestock. A good many cows were killed as a result, not to mention numerous sheep and an occasional pig; and to the horror of the farmers, the railroad refused to pay what the farmers considered fair damages. It was admitted that the railroad had killed livestock in the days of state ownership, but the men who operated the road then, being public officials reluctant to irritate any voters, had unhesitatingly paid full value for every animal killed; and it was held that some farmers made a good thing out of this, guiding ailing or decrepit animals onto the tracks and happily accepting the railroad's money in return.

Under private ownership, there was a different attitude. Superintendent Brooks held that the cattle were trespassers and their owners negligent, said that the railroad was under no legal liability whatever, and argued that if, in the interest of good will, the railroad paid half the appraised value for the animals killed, it would be doing the most anyone could ask. The farmers disagreed loudly, asserting that the offer to pay half-price was in itself an admission of liability and demanding that the railroad fence its right of way so that grazing cattle could be safe. The argument became heated, and there were incidents: a switch was jammed in one place, rails were removed in another, shots were fired at a train in the darkness, and on one stretch near Kalamazoo, rails were greased with tallow taken from the carcasses of cattle killed in action. So, suddenly, there was a nasty mess containing the possibility of serious trouble, and the trouble developed almost immediately.

To nobody's surprise, it came along a short stretch of line between Grass Lake and Michigan Center, in Jackson County. Here there was a soggy marsh, crossed by a railroad embankment, and cattle grazing on one side of the marsh found the embankment a convenient way to stroll over to grazing land on the other side—a thing that, in the obstinate way peculiar to cows, they were constantly doing. Naturally, a good many of them were killed, the farmers who owned them were demanding justice, and the railroad was refusing to pay; the farmers set up an informal but active organization to harass the railroad into paying up, and there was a marked rise in the incidents involving derailment, shooting, and general sabotage.

On its way into the history books, the whole business got blurred. It is remembered, if at all, mostly as an outbreak of rowdyism brought on by malcontents who had seen a lucrative racket broken by men whose only fault was that they insisted on running their railroad in a businesslike manner; by a huge effort, the railroad got the leading rowdies sent to prison, put the fear into the rest, and thereafter had no trouble. All of those elements were certainly present, but it seems clear that they tell only half the story: for the leader and principal strategist of the antirailroad movement was none other than Abel F. Fitch, leading citizen, man of substance, and moving spirit in the underground railroad, and although every man is entitled to go off half-cocked now and then, Fitch was assuredly no man to lead frontier strong boys in a meaningless assault on established property rights.

And as the trouble grew in size and scope during 1850 and early 1851, it became clear that the battle against the railroad had the strong support of the great majority of citizens in Jackson County. It was very hard to get local peace officers to arrest people for stoning or derailing trains, burning railroad fuel piles, or damaging bridges and culverts; and it was all but impossible to get Jackson County juries to convict men who were arrested for such offenses. The immediate cause at issue was the farmer's inability to get full compensation for cattle killed by the trains, but that was just the surface indicator. Underneath it, clearly enough, was deep resentment against the way the railroad had come to dominate affairs. It was a monopoly, it set rates as it chose (an especially sharp cause for complaint), its wage and hiring policies were considered unfair, it acted with a high hand on condemnation proceedings, and it seemed to have the courts right where it wanted them. Early in the struggle, when the railroad suggested that a test case on liability and valuation for killed cattle be taken to the state supreme court, with everybody agreeing to abide by whatever decision that court should reach, Fitch retorted contemptuously that judges had their price and could be bought as well as other men and said that the railroad was able to keep ordinary citizens from getting justice in any court. Public meetings, newspapers, and the state legislature voiced more and more the complaint that nobody was going to be safe until the greedy railroad monopoly was checked.

The real drift of things was shown in the summer of 1851, when a damage suit for stock killed by a train got to the state supreme court. As Fitch had foreseen, the court ruled for the railroad, holding that the road was bound neither by its charter nor by the common law to fence its right of way and could not be held responsible for damages unless actual negligence could be proved. But when it also ruled out the argument that the road's charter contained powers the legislature ought not to have granted, it suggested that this was a matter for the legislature, rather than the courts—a powerful hint that the real remedy for people oppressed by a monopoly lay with the elected law-makers. In time, this hint would be powerfully acted on.

Meanwhile, there was the dangerous tangle of violence, plots, bridge burning, and track destruction that went under the name of the Great Railroad Conspiracy: a flame flaring up on the surface to indicate the presence of highly flammable materials far underneath. Trains were stopped, rails were removed to cause derailments, a baggage car was burned (with U.S. mails in the baggage compartment), and when the railroad tried to prosecute a train-molester for high crimes, a local grand jury indicted one of the road's special police for perjury. A state constitutional convention adopted a section forbidding the legislature to pass individual acts of incorporation and outlawing special charters that granted monopolistic privileges, and the state legislature came perilously close to passing a law that would compel railroads to fence their tracks, build cattle guards at grade crossings, and equip all locomotives with whistles and bells. All in all, things were very bad, the railroad's freight station in Detroit was burned (by accident or by felonious intent), and passenger business fell off because people began to feel that it was not safe to ride Michigan Central trains.

It was unendurable, and the road hired a small army of private detectives to bring the saboteurs to justice. A complicating factor was the presence in small-town taverns along the right of way of irresponsible loud-mouth types who would drink too much and then talk freely about the dreadful things that were going to be done to the railroad. The detectives heard that men were going to set fire to the railroad's two passenger steamers on Lake Erie, that a train would be wrecked on the famous marsh embankment in such a way that all the passengers would be killed, and that railroad property in Jackson would be burned, even if half of Jackson got burned with it. There was no substance to most of this talk, but it undeniably made interesting reading.

The detectives collected a great mass of this sort of material, along with some more solid evidence, and in the spring of 1851 warrants were issued for the arrest of Fitch and forty-three others, charging them with a conspiracy to destroy the railroad and alleging a set of subsidiary offenses ranging from arson to counterfeiting. The central feature of the case, on which the whole prosecution would probably stand or fall, was the burning of the Michigan Central freight depot in Detroit four months earlier. Not only had the detectives found witnesses who purported to prove that Fitch and his aides had actively arranged to have this fire set: the fact that the fire had taken place in Detroit meant that the supposed conspirators would be tried there, and not in Jackson County, where sentiment ran so strongly in their favor.

The affair was theatrically managed—indeed, it could hardly have been handled more effectively, even today. Two special trains carrying deputy sheriffs (including one hundred specially deputized railroad hands) pulled into the Jackson County area in dead of night. The deputies broke up into squads and picked up Fitch and some three dozen others. These were taken to Detroit, and just when people there were going to work, the prisoners were marched through the center of town, two by two, escorted by twice their number of armed guards, to the county jail. The grand jury quickly returned a sheaf of indictments, there was a federal charge alleging destruction of U.S. mails and the use of counterfeit money, and the railroad filed civil suits against all hands for $150,000 damages. Bail was fixed at the wholly unattainable figure of $50,000 for each man . . . and, in short, having got them in Detroit, the authorities threw the book at them.

The press promptly joined the party, and the fantastic tales about plots to commit murder and create wholesale public catastrophe were given full publicity. It was widely charged that a "gang of desperadoes" [1] with members in several states was somehow responsible for the terrible things that had been done or attempted; the police were warned to be on the alert against arsonists still running at large, and the city authorities set up an elaborate night watch to protect downtown buildings from fire. The railroad people lent a hand, hiring at their own expense a special guard to surround the county jail and overawe any lawless folk who might attempt a rescue. Leading members of the Detroit bar were retained by the railroad to assist the county prosecutor, and general hysteria made it almost impossible for the defense to get any lawyers of stature. One lawyer of distinction, William A. Howard, did volunteer his services, remarking that the community stood in worse danger from a heartless corporation than from anything the defendants would ever do—and, for his pains, found himself widely denounced as an exponent of treason and a traitor to his class. Unfortunately, he was not actually skilled as a trial lawyer, but he did perform one notable service: he made a quick trip to Auburn, N.Y., and persuaded the famous William H. Seward to come to Detroit and take Fitch's case.

With Seward's arrival, the case ceases to be a simple matter of frontier toughs entrapped in the wreckage of a clumsy racket and takes on a significance more easily understood now than it was then—a trial of apparently lawless men whose story somehow provides a glimpse at fundamental injustice buried deep in the social order. Like all politicians, Seward was a man whose dimensions vary depending on his activity at any given moment and the point of view from which he is appraised. He could be a slippery customer serving his own ambition, and he could also

---

1. Charles Hirschfeld, "The Great Railroad Conspiracy," in *Michigan History,* XXXVI, no. 2:147.

be a man nobly devoted to high principle, and sometimes he could be both at once, so that it is not always easy to get him in focus. In 1851, he was a member of the United States Senate, famous for his opposition to human slavery and his talk of a Higher Law; he was also known as a lawyer who now and then responded to the impulse to place himself on the side of the culprits society was most anxious to condemn. In 1846, for instance, he fought hard for a nobody named Bill Freeman, of Auburn, who was the head man in a singularly brutal and senseless mass murder case.

Son of a former slave, Bill Freeman was a casual laborer who was sent to prison for horse-stealing and was savagely beaten by his keepers. One of them beat him over the head with a plank, breaking the plank and breaking Bill Freeman's head as well, inflicting permanent damage on a brain that had not been in very good shape to begin with. Released from prison in 1845, Bill apparently spent most of his waking hours brooding on his evil fate, and he seems to have worked it out that somebody owed him money for the hard labor he had put in while a convict; and in the spring of 1846, triggered by heaven knows just what, he went forth with a butcher knife and killed the first four people he met: a farmer, the farmer's wife and small child, and the wife of a neighbor who had the bad luck to wander onto the scene just when Freeman was at his peak. He was caught, thrown in jail in Auburn, narrowly escaped lynching, and was obviously slated for a quick trip to the gallows.

This was in Seward's home town. Seward had political ambitions, and "Crazy Bill," as Freeman was known, had a one-way ticket to nowhere with a greased noose to help him along; but a minister in Auburn, moved by something a little above the popular level, made bold to ask the question: "Is not society in some degree accountable for this sad catastrophe?" [2] Seward felt that the question was aimed at him, answered it in the affirmative, volunteered to act as Freeman's defense counsel without pay, and went to work in a hopeless cause. He argued that

2. James Taylor Dunn and Louis C. Jones, "Crazy Bill Had a Down Look," *American Heritage,* VI, no. 5:108.

Crazy Bill simply was not mentally competent and ought not to be held accountable for deeds that a competent man should answer for; and although he lost and saw Freeman sentenced to be hanged, he fought the case through to a higher court and won a reversal of sentence. Crazy Bill was granted a new trial, but he died in jail before the trial could be held. A post-mortem examination indicated that his brain had been hideously damaged by the prison beatings, and nobody in particular had won anything out of all of this, except that Senator Seward had more or less made a point. And now he was in Detroit, taking up the cause of Abel Fitch and assorted lesser lights.

The cases did not exactly run parallel. Fitch was not a drifter with a defective brain, but a man of substance who could afford to retain a good lawyer; Seward got $2,000 for his work in this case, and the heat he faced here was nothing like the murderous fury that had surrounded the case of Crazy Bill. Yet there was a certain similarity, far down inside, possibly because a corporation, when its blood is up, can be as implacable as an infuriated populace; and in each case, an attempt to punish a crime of violence led society itself to sit in the dock as a co-defendant.

Seward quickly discovered that it was impossible to get Fitch or any of the others released on bail. The $50,000 bail originally set was plainly excessive, and Seward managed to get it reduced to $20,000, which Fitch was able to meet; but this helped not at all, because there was also a $50,000 bail bond required for each of the defendants in the railroad's civil suit for damages, and he could not get this cut at all. He found himself before long urging the court to show "a proper sense of its obligations to God and humanity, and love of liberty for the oppressed under all circumstances," [3] but the eloquence did no good, and all hands stayed in jail. The jail was overcrowded, the food served was miserable, the summer was very hot, and some of the defendants were in bad health to begin with—Fitch himself suffered from what was then called dyspepsia and probably was a case of stomach ulcers; and two of his fellow defendants died before the trial was fairly begun.

3. Hirschfeld, "The Great Railroad Conspiracy," p. 155.

The trial lasted for three months. Nearly 500 witnesses were heard, and at this distance it seems impossible to determine exactly what was proved. Early in the game, the court ruled that, although the defendants were being tried solely for burning the Detroit freight station, things said and done in Jackson County months earlier should be taken into consideration if they tended to show a general conspiracy to harm the railroad. This meant that all of the blood-and-thunder tavern talk about wrecking trains, killing passengers, and destroying everything the railroad owned could be recited before the jury, which very likely was greatly impressed thereby—or, possibly, greatly confused. A modern reader is likely to conclude that this must have been one of the most boring, meaningless trials ever held—except that real people were involved, with a real prison cell perfectly visible on the far side of all the courtroom maneuvering, and death itself now and then reaching into the squalid jail where the prisoners were lodged. Before the trial ended, Abel Fitch himself died, saying solemnly "I shall die a martyr to liberty," and then, more humanly, calling to his wife: "Amanda, it is hard to part—I die of a broken heart." [4] It developed that, having paid practically all of the legal expenses for his co-defendants, he had bankrupted his estate. By the time the case went to the jury, late in September, only thirty-two defendants remained.

The jury took nine hours to reach its verdict, convicting twelve men and exonerating the rest. The judge lectured the convicted men sternly on the error of their ways, and then handed out two ten-year sentences, six eight-year sentences, and set five-year terms for the rest. The great railroad conspiracy case was closed, with nothing much settled—except that the matter did not rest, but sent widening ripples down through the state's history for some years to come.

For it was clear enough that the whole sorry business had been a logical ending to a process that had been going on from the earliest days. Unrestrained exploitation of natural resources, from beavers through pine trees to iron and copper ore, had led naturally enough to unrestrained exploitation of human beings.

---

4. Hirschfeld, "The Great Railroad Conspiracy," p. 173.

The railroad monopoly had been wholly ruthless, as if the monopolistic charter given it by the state had relieved it of all responsibility for its acts: it could set rates as it chose, favoring this place and handicapping that one, it could drive its tracks across rich farming land without a thought for the harm that might be done to animals or people who crossed the path; and when men made protest, it could pursue them through the courts and into state's prison as if nothing but vengeance mattered. Part of the state had been given to this monopoly to use as it saw fit, and here was the result. When Seward told the jury that, if any conspiracy existed, it was a conspiracy by railroad officials to jail people who disapproved of railroad policies, he summed it up neatly enough.

Except for its immediate victims, this conspiracy was a total failure. Opposition to the monopoly spread all across the Central's territory in the years following the trial, and clearly enough it was no longer based on complaints that locomotives ran over cows: it was fired by a deep, passionate determination to get this monopoly back under the people's control and compel it to accept responsibility for its acts, and the Central's officers quickly realized what was up. They became conciliatory, calling on the governor to pardon the men they had had sent to prison; and four years after the trial ended, pardons were issued. Not long afterward, the legislature acted; laws were passed making railroads responsible for all cattle killed where the tracks were not fenced or where suitable protective measures were not taken at grade crossings, engines were required to sound whistles or bells when approaching such crossings, and suddenly the wrongs that had seemed to spark the farmers' uprising had been set right. A little later, a general railroad incorporation law was passed, the monopoly was ended, and it was no longer possible for the Central to keep other railroads from entering its territory. The state even asserted a slight measure of control over the rate-making process. The millennium was still a long way off, but at least a step had been taken. In a dim, uncertain, and not wholly conscious way, the state had resolved that exploitation of resources ought to be under some sort of restraint—an idea that was totally new.

As a matter of fact a political revolution was going on, and the sign and symbol of it suddenly became visible at Jackson, the very center of the great railroad conspiracy. On July 6, 1854, in an open grove on the edge of town, several thousand dissidents met to take political action. They were oddly assorted: abolitionists, free soilers, antislavery Democrats, conscience Whigs, men who were drifting into populism from one cause or another—all of these met, orated, resolved, and wound up by forming the Republican party.

This party looked very different then from the way it looked a century later. It began by bringing together men profoundly discontented with the shape things were taking in the middle of the nineteenth century—men who had very little in common except a growing belief that a society to which so much had been given was bound at last to ask: For whose good was all of this meant? There were the Whigs, the ultrarespectables, men who believed devoutly in freedom, but tended to lack sympathy with those who lacked means, breeding, and an Anglo-Saxon ancestry; and there were Democrats, skeptical about the notion that freedom had anything to do with the black man but instinctively fearful that men of wealth were conspiring to curtail the rights of whites; and they were joining hands because the pressures of the times were growing irresistible. Chattel slavery was far away, but from its evils came the dark drifting mist of fugitives whom law-abiding men somehow had to help along the road to freedom, even though the law said that this was wrong; much closer home, there was an injustice that led the same law-abiders to side with men who burned railroad stations and derailed passenger trains; and it was not wholly by accident that these folk met under the oaks at Jackson. Not yet expressed, not yet wholly realized, was the deep truth that, ultimately, oppression is all of one piece, so that to attack it in one place is to commit one's self to attack it everywhere.

Now the noteworthy point is that the men who were coming to this conclusion were men to whom much had been given—vast forests, deep veins of ore, rich farms and orchards and fisheries—and their assertion of the rights of man took place against a background of unmeasured abundance. The state was not yet a man's lifetime away from its uncombed territorial beginnings, but it had already given men the habit of expecting the utmost. A new force had been turned loose in the world, the conviction that man does not have to be a loser. There was more than enough of everything to go around; from which it followed, or seemed to follow, that if anyone did not get his share someone somewhere must be getting a great deal too much. A belief in unlimited resources simply creates a set of unlimited desires. This is the incalculable, explosive fact that lies just below the surface in American life.

That the political party born of discontent with the power held by men of wealth eventually became the chosen instrument of the wealthiest of all should surprise no one. This party, to repeat, was created by men who had won some privileges and hoped to win more, or at least to defend the ones they had; quite naturally, it finally came to speak for those whose privileges, appetites, and determination were greatest. And its creation also came, very neatly, just as a wholly new resource mightier than all of the others came into play. Men now discovered what they could do with machinery, and man's mechanical ingenuity—his power to manipulate things, to do quickly and easily what had always been done slowly and with immense effort—suddenly gave him the lever and fulcrum of Archimedes. Presently he could move the world, and presently he would do it.

How all of this came about would make a very long story indeed. For various reasons, it had particularly explosive effects in Michigan, and possibly the state ought to inscribe the year 1876 in its calendar as a great year of portents. Two people in that year saw mechanical devices, got ideas from them, eventually put the ideas into effect, and did much to change the state's development.

The first was young Scott Gerish, who visualized the lumber-moving potential of the narrow-gauge railway locomotive he glimpsed at Philadelphia's Centennial Exposition, put the idea into practice, and revolutionized the lumber industry: Gerish's little idea knocked from fifty to a hundred years off the life of Michigan's forests, immeasurably shortening the distance between wilderness frontier and industrial era.

The second person to have a significant vision that year was a boy named Henry Ford, who was riding along a road near Detroit in a buggy with his father when a steam threshing-machine engine came chugging along. This engine was a type of steam tractor, strong enough to haul a heavy-duty threshing machine from one farm to another and adaptable enough to power the machine on arrival. This morning, it seems to have been going along the road with no threshing machine in tow, and it was the first time in his life that young Master Ford ever saw a self-propelled vehicle on the public highway. The sight fascinated him, and that moment there was born in his mind a vision of vehicles small enough, light enough, and maneuverable enough to take people by road wherever they wanted to go. This vision found its lodging in precisely the right spot, and eventually Henry Ford did something about it.

By this coincidence—machines seen in the centennial year by just the right people—the lumber industry and the auto industry are symbolically linked, and Gerish and Ford become part of the same progression. Actually, there is more than a symbolic linkage. The lumber barons, unintentionally but effectively, prepared the way for the men who were going to make autos: by piling up the necessary capital, by stimulating the immigration that created a pool of available factory hands, and by helping to develop industries that could take easily and naturally to the production of autos when the time came. In its beginnings—indeed, all through its lusty youth and beyond—the manufacture of autos was dangerously speculative, frowned on by eastern capitalists and for that matter by middle western bankers as well. The men who made money out of the pine forests were, first of all, chance-takers; they had a good thing going, and they grew rich thereby, but they always knew that a bad turn of luck—a couple of mild winters, for instance—could put them in the red, perhaps put them out of business altogether. They were speculators by nature, their trade was born of the frontier's boom-or-bust philosophy, and to put surplus money into a business that might prove to be no business at all was nothing they were not used to. The deep-wood lumber trade kept the frontier alive in Michigan right into the industrial age, which created exactly the condition in which this new industry could find birth and vigorous growth. Basically, the auto industry was a frontier venture. That it grew up in Michigan was wholly natural.

There were side effects. The lumber boom had created a carriage trade—people prosperous enough to ride around in horse-drawn carriages—and it had also created carriage factories to meet the demand created by this trade. These factories clustered about places like Flint and Detroit, where the needed specialty timber was easy to obtain, and when the time came it was simple enough to have them make horseless carriages. The requirements of sawmills, logging railroads, and mining camps had brought machine shops and foundries into being, downstate, and had built up a corps of skilled workers who knew how to operate them. By supplying both the building timber and the paying freight, the lumber trade had developed a ship-building industry along the Detroit, St. Clair, and Saginaw rivers, and as iron and steel began to replace wood in the shipyards, a number of the builders began to turn out small craft; and so there were factories that developed and built the internal combustion engines that would power the small craft. Altogether, the bits and pieces needed for auto production were all in place, ready to be used.

But the important thing was the frame of mind: the readiness to take a chance, coupled with the belief that the sky is the limit, and an intangible something born of the reliance on resources that are believed to be inexhaustible. That belief, of course, had long since passed into folklore and was never held by the long-headed men who hired the land-lookers, grub-staked the prospectors, and knew how to figure costs, depreciation allowances, and prospective profits as well as any men who ever lived. But operating in a field where the basic resource was supposed to be unlimited and was, in fact, unlimited for the short time of a profit-taker's heyday had created an attitude that affected even the canniest. This attitude survived the death of the forests and the deep depletion of the ore bodies, and actually it came down to the present time stronger than ever before. The only change is in the nature of the inexhaustible resource.

Somewhere along the line, man made a right-angle turn and

believed that he had found a resource that would be truly and forever inexhaustible—technology. The sky was still the limit, more now than ever before; and it was man himself who held it suspended, high over all. On this belief, this state, and the nation, and the rest of the world, must try to get through the twentieth century.

11

Master of His Fate

T is one state out of fifty, but somehow its story helps to sum up the whole. Here, perhaps more clearly than in most places, can be seen the enormous increase in the speed of society's movement, the pressures that come when a society adjusted to one era is suddenly compelled to shape itself to an entirely new one, the torment of modern man torn by the astounding discovery that the things he makes have taken charge of his life. Living in memory of an interesting past and imagining himself to be relaxing in the warmth of a long afternoon, man finds himself facing a terrifying dawn—and it seems to be a little too much for him. Without intending anything of the kind, he discovers that he is involved in an enormous revolution, simply because the power in his hands is so vast that its mere existence turns the world upside down. Michigan certainly did not cause this to happen, but it shows a good deal about *how* it happened. Here is the slice of modern life, ready to go to the lab for the biopsy.

In the beginning, there was the abundance. On the continent, in the nation, in the state, man discovered that he lived in the midst of overflowing plenty. From animals to fertile soil, from great forests to deep veins of ore and mountains of useful minerals, there was so much of everything that whole generations based thought and action on the faith that there would never be an end to it. This abundance stimulated the desire to consume it, and, at exactly this moment, the ability to make and use power-driven machinery was itself greatly expanded—inevitably, because boundless desire acting on unlimited resources demands and finally creates unlimited technological capacity. What happens when boundless desire and unlimited capacity no longer have inexhaustible resources to work on will doubtless be most instructive.

Fully characteristic of a society whose desires became ever more insistent as the possibility of satisfying them increased was a demand for more speed and flexibility of movement. In the beginning, the wilderness could not even be entered until men were able to get past its natural barriers, its roadless bogs and tangled woods and the mysterious lights and shadows that masked its promises. If they were to make towns and farms, in place of mere trading posts, they had to be able to come and go easily; at every point in the process of development, it was abundantly clear that not merely progress, but survival itself depended on the ability to move people and their goods freely. The bitter tumult of the Great Railroad Conspiracy was simply a declaration that this freedom was essential. A society founded on progressive exploitation of the earth's riches must be fluid; to be rigid would be to miss all manner of opportunities. Furthermore, it obviously would not pay to grow rich by creating a wasteland if one had to go on living in the wasteland after the wealth had been exhausted. The land of abundance could be enjoyed only if there were complete freedom to move about in it.

Progress, in other words, was from the first equated with improved transportation. Successive improvements were a law of life, each one making all former improvements obsolete. Nothing cost too much if it meant greater ease of movement, and nothing was too expensive to discard if someone came up with a new device. The enormous appeal of the narrow-gauge logging road lay in the fact that it was so obviously a temporary thing. Once it had served its brief purpose, it could be picked up, carried off, sold for scrap, or simply thrown away. Only the standard-sized railroads were supposed to be permanent; and in the end, it was seen that they were not permanent, either, but were subject to the inexorable wastage imposed by the blind devotion of the society that had built them. The only thing that would endure was progress itself.

Or so men believed. It becomes clear that this was, above all other things, a *prodigal* society; inevitably so, no doubt, in view of the base on which it was built. The bounty was going to last forever, and, if you threw something away, you could always replace it with something better. It was all for free, in the beginning, anyway, and if it cost something, that did not matter, because the result was all anyone needed to think about. In this new world, man could go where he chose, with a freedom no one but the raiding centaurs from the Asian steppes had ever known before. In a surprising way, Étienne Brulé turns out to have been the pace-setter. He went where he wanted to go and had immense new experiences. Unfortunately, to be sure, he died of it.

So if there ever was a state qualified to lead the way into the great age of the automobile, it was Michigan.

The automobile, of course, was not invented in Michigan, and its development might easily have come somewhere else. It remains true, however, that the development did take place here and that the great case history of what happens to a people dedicated to the automobile has been recorded here. It is not possible to tell the story of this state without putting the internal combustion engine, the rubber tire, and the white desert-ribbons of the concrete highway on to the center of the stage for the grand finale.

The automobile itself is a symbol, rather than a cause. It accelerated change beyond measure, but the real change had begun earlier. This frontier state dedicated to the quick extraction of wealth that had been there from the beginning had developed explosive qualities before the automobile was anything more than a noisy fixed idea for a few tinkering mechanics. Detroit was to become the capital city of the world-on-wheels, a pillar of cloud by day and fire by night to mark the path that must be followed, but it did not go that way by accident.

At the time of the Civil War, Detroit was a thriving but still companionable small city in a home-spun middle west; it had 45,000 inhabitants, and although it had busy docks, shipyards, shops, and small factories, it still had the look of its early days, and its base rested squarely on forests, mines, waterways, and railroads. Its appearance would have surprised Cadillac, who had brought it into being in the first place, but he could have found his way around in it.

Then the center of gravity began to shift. Perhaps this was because of the immense convulsion of the Civil War, which changed so many things so greatly, or perhaps it was just something that grew out of the vast ferment caused by energy, ambition, and wealth working together in a society that still had a frontier outlook; whatever it was, there was a change in character and in tempo. There was a steady, year-by-year development of what was obviously becoming an industrial belt across the southern third of the state. In 1860, this area had just under 3,500 manufacturing establishments with a total invested capital of $28,000,000; at the turn of the century, there were more than 16,000 factories, representing an investment of $284,000,000. Detroit had burst its seams; even in the 'nineties, it began to boast that it was now the fifteenth city in size in all the United States, and when the federal census-takers counted heads in 1900, they found that there were more than 250,000 Detroiters. This was no longer the companionable little city of the old days. It was a city with muscle, moving at full speed into the twentieth century.

The situation was still fluid. There was no key industry dominating the whole. Bigness was not yet the order of the day. Detroit made all sorts of things—carriages, paints, stoves, pharmaceuticals, ships, hardware, railroad cars, and shoes—and although it was beginning to make automobiles, this activity was of no particular importance. The average businessman was an independent operator, not the executive of a corporation; the average wage-earner belonged to no union (as a heritage from the lumber-baron days, Michigan had a powerful open-shop tradition), and in a great many instances, he had no special skills. Detroit had problems, and it worried about them, but when it tried to confront them, it found itself facing the familiar ogres of capitalism's formative days.

Thus, in the 1890s, times were bad, with the kind of recession that men not yet addicted to soothing euphemisms bluntly called a panic. Detroit had for mayor a man named Hazen S. Pingree, a solid, mildly eccentric shoe manufacturer (he carried bits of salt codfish in his pockets, munching on them in moments of stress) who took office in 1890 and quickly came to the conclusion that the people were being cheated. Inasmuch as Detroit, like virtually all other American cities of that day, was ruthlessly governed by corrupt machine politicians of the old school, Pingree was undoubtedly right, and he tried to do something about it. He is remembered now largely because, when unemployment became widespread and jobless workers were going hungry, he started a city-wide campaign to turn vacant lots into vegetable gardens; he was widely derided for it, but the campaign was actually a huge success, and many jobless workers raised the potatoes and beans that kept their families from starving during the thin times.

Campaigning against civic oppression, Pingree struggled for lower utility rates, better transportation (that leitmotif of Michigan's story), reforms in the election laws, free silver, and antitrust action. Some of these causes, to be sure, were not in the purview of any mayor, but in others he won his fight, driving down the rates for gas and establishing a municipal electric plant that had lasting effect. He finally saw that he needed a wider field than any city hall could command, and he ran for governor and was elected—only to find, at last, that he had picked the wrong causes, or at least that he had picked them at the wrong times.

To argue for free silver was simply to ride William Jennings Bryan's coattails to defeat, and to raise the trust-buster's banner was to plunge into a live mine field before Theodore Roosevelt had charted a path across it. Pingree failed, at last, and in a final speech, he summed up what he had learned: "In order to secure the full support of those who consider themselves 'the better classes' the Governor and other high officials must do nothing to antagonize the great corporations and the wealthy people." Then he turned to dark prophecy: "I make the prediction that, unless those in charge and in whose hands legislation is reposed do not change the present system of inequality, in less than a quarter of a century there will be a bloody revolution in this great country of ours." [1]

Tides were beginning to move in 1900 that no politician could be expected to detect, and if a revolution lay ahead, it was of a sort that was beyond anyone's imagination when the century was new. It is noteworthy that Pingree chose one target before it had fully taken shape. Again and again he spoke out against what he called "the corporationists," meaning chiefly the combinations of capital confronted by a reform mayor—the utilities that kept rates up and services down and corrupted public servants by bribery or more subtle pressures. These forces were real enough, but at least they were out where a fighting mayor could get at them, and their power was not quite earth-moving, after all. What had not yet developed—not in Michigan—was the corporate wealth that reached out to control the unheard-of power that is born of technological proficiency. Here was the greatest power that ever existed on earth, coming into shape not so much off-stage as beyond ready understanding. Pingree and men like him could not be expected to see it; at best, they could prepare the ground for a generation that would have a more sophisticated vision.

For in Pingree's day, corporate wealth, in Michigan's industrial belt, had not got very far. When the twentieth century began, less than fourteen percent of the state's industrial establishments were corporately owned. About twice that many were owned by partnerships, and all the rest were owned by individuals. This situation, to be sure, was changing fast. The self-sufficiency reflected by the figures of 1900 was in rapid decline. Industry was becoming more complex; surest sign of all, urbanization was growing at a constantly increasing rate. But the change was not yet entirely visible. It was just beginning to pick up speed when the era of the automobile began— and before anybody quite knew how it happened, the accelerator had been pressed all the way down to the floor.

Years later, when the full scope of the change brought by the automobile was obvious to everybody, people who tried to ex-

1. Warner and Vanderhill, *A Michigan Reader*, pp. 95–96.

plain why this device was introduced and perfected just then instead of at some other time found that the riddle was both ridiculously easy and beyond explanation. The thing could not have happened earlier, because the world's technology was not sufficiently advanced; no stretch of the imagination can show the men of 1870, for instance, making a self-propelled road vehicle that would transform the nature of human civilization. But why were so many talented mechanics, tinkerers, and inventors, in America and in Europe, working on it around the year 1900? Perhaps the best answer is the one given by Hiram Percy Maxim, himself one of the pioneers: "Because it had become apparent that civilization was ready for the mechanical vehicle." [2]

A mystic's answer: here was an idea whose time had come—implying that there is a rhythm, a mindless but intent groping-for, going on below the surface in human society that leads men to see with eyes not their own, to plan with a mind they do not consciously command or obey. All very true, perhaps, but not something you can easily weigh, measure, or appraise. Still, it did happen; in the course of a decade, the making of automobiles ceased to be a risky experiment and became an industry, and the soul and center of it were in southern Michigan, with Detroit clearly dominant. Halfway through the first decade of the twentieth century, the New York automobile show saw orders placed for 12,000 cars; fully half of these cars were ordered from Detroit, and a boom that would shatter all sound barriers was in the making.

The potentialities were limitless, for making cars and for making money, and men took advantage of them with whole-souled energy. However it got started, it seems clear that the whole bewildering process came out of the heart and center of the society that had grown up between the lakes and the forests and the iron-shod hills. It was a society born to exploit: to seize the main chance at any cost, to take advantage of every opportunity, to assert control over the environment itself and work

2. Allan Nevins, *Ford: the Times, the Man, the Company;* 3 vols. (New York: Charles Scribner's Sons, 1954), I:133.

unending change without bothering to reflect that the changes thus wrought would in the end change the lives of whole generations of men.

On top of this, it was ideally prepared to develop a new industry, which, confronting a market that expanded by geometric progression, was obliged to devise a production system that could expand in the same way. To do this, it not only needed leaders who understood the ultimate possibilities of machinery; it needed a labor force that was both leaderless, energetic, and handy with tools—men sturdy enough to stand the gaff and docile enough to do as they were told. Detroit became center of the new industry for many reasons, among them its possession of the kinds of factories that could easily be converted to automobile production and the shops, foundries, and bits-and-pieces plants that would turn out wheels, gears, motors, and parts; but one factor as important as any of these was the powerful and, at the moment, unbreakable tradition of the open shop.

This developed naturally enough. Just when the new industry was getting started, the Great Lakes area was running into trouble. In Michigan, especially, the lumber industry was getting to the end of the line, the camps were closing, lumber towns were dying, and the mills that employed so many men were tying their whistles down, exhausting the last steam in their boilers with long-drawn, mournful wails, and shipping saws, edgers, and conveyors off to the Far West or the Deep South. The men who had worked in camps and mills drifted to the cities, looking for work—drifted automatically, inevitably, because there obviously was not going to be any work in the cut-over country where they had always lived. They came by the thousands to places like Detroit and Flint, and when they took jobs, they had no labor union tradition to sustain them— the lumber barons had suppressed unionism with a heavy hand.

At the same time, the Michigan industrial belt, like those in other states, was pulling immigrants from abroad. More and more, these came from eastern Europe and, like the former sawmill hands, brought with them no habit of labor organization. In the Detroit area, to be sure, a good many of the skilled workers were unionized, but one of the oddities of this new industry was its ability to make increasing use of men who were not machinists or metal workers at all, but who could easily be taught to go on the production line and perform certain routine operations. On top of everything else, most of these men believed that they were living in an open society. Individually-owned plants still existed—there was, after all, the case of Henry Ford—and in every company, there were in high positions men who had come up from the ranks. It was still possible to believe in the gospel according to Horatio Alger.

But the important thing here is not the story of the industry's growth pains, of how its founding fathers got along or what happened to its workers. The auto industry was and is the crest of a great wave that is still driving on toward the beach. It shows what can happen. We are going somewhere at a prodigious rate, and the chief point in examining our past is the chance that we may find out where we are headed and what is taking us there. The Detroit story can be instructive.

The automobile makers assuredly did not invent mass production, although it sometimes seems as if the whole thing had been a Detroit idea. Other manufacturers had long since discovered that a fantastic output can be reached when standardized, simplified, and completely interchangeable parts flow together on a production line so arranged that it operates without lost time or waste motion. What Detroit did was subject this process to a forced draft, because, after the experimental years were over, it appeared that the public wanted more automobiles than the industry could produce. No matter how many automobiles were made, demand kept ahead of supply. It was necessary to produce as much as possible as rapidly as possible, to do this was to produce more cheaply, which forced retail prices down and brought new customers into the market—and all in all, here was the manufacturer's New Jerusalem, coming down out of Heaven arrayed like a bride. In all history, nothing like this had ever been seen before.

The direct results were devastating. In the course of one generation, the whole population was put on wheels. People suddenly found that they had complete, unfettered mobility, restrained only by the danger of multiple-stage collisions—which meant that the entire transportation system was recast. Inasmuch as the whole organization of modern society depends on the means people use to get themselves and their goods from here to there, this meant changes in the whole social structure—dramatic, fundamental changes, affecting everything each human being does from birth to death. All of this was brought about with complete social irresponsibility. Nothing was planned; people conditioned to want fluidity of movement above all other things just reached out and took it when they got the chance. Quite early in the game, they learned that too much fluidity can cause paralysis: in other words, that when too many automobiles try to use the same roads there are monstrous traffic jams. The remedy, of course, was to build more and more roads, which in turn called out more and more automobiles and created larger and more expensive traffic jams, which compelled the building of still more roads, which . . .

This mobile society turned out to be the most prodigal the world had ever seen. Every man can be put on wheels only if nobody stops to figure out what it is all going to cost. (The machines themselves can be built cheaply enough, heaven knows: it is using them, and adjusting to them, that is so expensive.) There had been abundant mental preparation for all of this. Here was the state that gave away great forests and iron ranges, with the carefree liberality of a sailor on shore leave, in order to get railroads built, laying steel trails up and down and across a wilderness in the abiding faith that everything would be justified in a great tomorrow. While they were new, and while they lasted, these steel trails changed the countryside and the people, raising this place to the heights and dooming that place to a lasting decline, exercising these powers not because anybody in particular had worked out a program, but simply because man ultimately has to adapt himself and his institutions to his manner of moving about on the face of the earth.

As railroads were built, so were highways, with no eye for costs. The concrete ribbons grew longer and wider every year, and their loops became more and more convoluted, and the only thing that mattered was to create more of them and extend them past every hill and across every valley. The railroads were driven into bankruptcy and began to vanish utterly, and highway-building became almost a religious observance. It seemed advisable to throw a highway bridge across the Straits of Mackinac, although an earlier generation would have considered this both impossible and unnecessary; it was done, at a cost of a hundred million or thereabouts; autos rolled across it, and, in increasing thousands, the bridge itself became an object of adoration, with thousands of people driving up just to have a look at it. Mackinaw City, its original reason for being having evaporated, became a fantastic tourists' city of motels and restaurants and curio shops.

The society that did all of this had obviously committed itself to movement, regardless of cost. The oceans of fuel used come from half the world away, and it may be time to reflect on their eventual exhaustion and on social anarchy that may result when a highly mobile society abruptly finds that it cannot move.

The problem is characteristic. The whole organization of society is keyed to a means of transportation that must, some day, in the familiar phrase, run out of gas. And Michigan, where the age of the automobile came to its fullest flowering, is a state that grew up in the belief that abundance is forever. Men gabbled about inexhaustible forests and unlimited ores, right up to the moment when further self-deception became impossible. They adjusted their whole social structure to a force whose life span was similarly limited and kept from worrying unduly by increasing reliance on the faith that sustains the modern world— a faith not in the goodness of God, but in the endless ingenuity of man. This faith demands total orthodoxy, although it creates its own skeptics as it goes along.

Men who gain salvation by their own ingenuity often behave in unexpected ways. Sighting along the old familiar guidelines, Governor Pingree predicted revolution in a quarter-century. What finally happened was not quite what was anticipated, although it did represent a remarkable turn-over for certain old beliefs and privileges. The semiskilled, utterly unorganized men who did routine things along the production lines realized, presently, that the very existence of the all-powerful new industry depended on those production lines, which in turn depended wholly on the men who tended them—who consequently held a power no one ever thought wage earners could ever get unless they left the factory and rushed to the barricades. Instead of going to the barricades, these men simply stayed in the factory, picking up and perfecting an odd new tactic known as the sit-down strike. Before long, the one-time center of the militant open shop had become the center of a disciplined, militant unionism such as Detroit had never dreamed of.

Like so many other things that have happened lately, this was unplanned. The giant corporations quite unintentionally brought giant unions in their train, and the corporate leaders undoubtedly thought for a time that Governor Pingree's revolution was indeed upon them in all its horror. Actually, the revolution that finally came was beyond the understanding either of the corporate leaders or of the avowed revolutionists, who somehow believed that a time when all institutions collapsed would be precisely the time when the most rigid patterns of formulated orthodoxy would be followed. The dialectic of the left was as pointless as that of the right, because when the new world began to take shape, it did not look like anything either side had anticipated. All that was really clear was that, because men had greater powers than they had ever expected to have, the things they did would have incalculable effects.

Thus the automobile is catalyst for a series of forces that are destroying the established social order. Fittingly enough, this is clearly visible in that fabulous city of magnificent beginnings, Detroit itself.

Detroit is of the essence of the twentieth century. And yet, if a reflective person sits down to ponder about it, he is likely to find himself meditating about the deserted cities of the ancient Mayas, far down in Mexico.

These cities have been in ruins since time was young, and the descendants of the people who built them know nothing much about them, except that they vaguely suspect that they are haunted. They contain survivals of a mighty architecture, with shining towers rising above the green surf of a shoreless jungle, monuments to a faith that once led Stone-Age men to test themselves, apparently, just a little beyond their capacity. These cities pose a riddle that goes beyond mere puzzlement over the as-tounding skills that went into their construction. It is hard for a modern man to understand why they were built at all. They ap-pear to have been ceremonial centers, elaborate places for rites of worship or government, but it does not seem that they were places where very many people lived. They contain temples but no houses, statues and paintings and memorials to the mighty ones (of this world or the next) but no shops or markets. If they drew multitudes in, now and then—as they unquestionably did: some of them are large, and somebody went to great trouble to design and build them—they sent them all away again after a short time. Sooner or later, the student finds himself wondering what they were for and suspecting that the sheer immobile weight of them finally dragged the people who built them down to defeat. For all of these cities, sooner or later, were deserted.

A long way off, to be sure, and Yucatan is not much like Michigan, except for the coincidence that both are peninsulas. But at this moment, Detroit cannot really be defined or de-scribed. In one sense, it is a hollow shell; in another, it is a state of mind; in still another, it is a growing section of the state of Michigan, spraddling out over what very recently was good farming country, planting the most startling skyscrapers and modernistic factories where nobody had ever planted anything but corn, up to a year or so ago. Where the heart of the city is depends on who you are, what your job is, and where you sleep; it is likely to be miles away from anything men would have recognized a few years earlier as part of Detroit. Over and over again, crossing level green fields to find a cluster of soaring towers reaching for the distant sky, you find yourself thinking: Magnificent—but of course no one really lives here.

The Mayas at least had something in mind, even though we do not know what it was, when they built their cities. Today's cities, in the very heart of automobile land, were built while men were thinking about something else. They built the au-tomobile; and the automobile has become the instrument through which the whole face of the earth is changed. It changes because men can go where they will. Men who can go where they will look for more comfortable places to work and play and live; in the finest tradition of this land of milk and honey and riches-for-the-taking, they use up what they have, throw the husk away, and go on to fairer fields.

Nowhere is this so frighteningly visible as in Detroit. There is a certain pattern handed down from earlier generations. The forests were used hard and at last used up, and the sawmill towns that grew so great fell ill and some of them died outright, so that the former lumber country is spotted with ghost towns, where blank windows look out of decaying, paintless houses, and weeds grow on docks and in empty railroad yards. The mines were used in the same way, and the mining country has ghost towns of its own, with the gaunt buildings that once housed pit-head machinery standing over the deep shafts that go down to darkness. And now there are the great industrial cities with blank windows and empty houses of their own.

Detroit is not really a ghost town, of course, because many hundreds of thousands of people still live there. In a sense, they have to live there. Some of them are tied down by jobs. Others have invested their savings in homes or small businesses and will lose if they sell out to move elsewhere. And a great many have simply lost or never gained the mobility that is modern man's great acquired characteristic. To all intents and purposes, public transportation has died, and the man who cannot afford transportation of his own has to stay put. When everyone else goes off to some place where life is nicer, he has to make the best of what cannot be carried off, and the best may not be very good. A city that contains so many people who would move out if they could is not likely to have a robust community spirit, and so crime rates go up, and there is a great increase in homicides, the traffic in drugs thrives, the relief rolls are all scabby with people who have given up, and, under the surface, the city suffers progressive physical and spiritual decay. It becomes a less pleasant place to live and work, and so more of the people who can move out do so, and the gap between those who move and those who stay becomes wider and wider, the mutual estrangement, more and more bitter.

Tocqueville saw American democracy when it was younger and simpler, and back in the 1830s, he remarked that, before long, "Man will be less and less able to produce, of himself alone, the commonest necessaries of life." A society whose lusty tradition of individualism and firm belief in the equality of all men were both based on that frontier ability is likely to flounder when conditions change, and Tocqueville went on to draw a somber conclusion: "Among the laws which rule human societies there is one which seems to be more precise and clear than all others. If men are to remain civilised, or to become so, the art of associating together must grow and improve in the same ratio in which the equality of conditions is increased." [3]

Hazen Pingree saw it the same way and feared that a revolution was coming "because of the present system of inequality."

It is neither the increased mobility nor the ingrained prodigal wastage that causes the real trouble. Under everything else, there is a loss of "the art of associating together," and an increase in "the present system of inequality," and from these comes darkness. So perhaps there are fixed grades and classes of men, after all, even in the land of promise, with eternal enmity dividing the halves of society; and perhaps it was a long whisper such as this that caused everyone to let those Mayan cities go back to the jungle.

It is a fatal time to lose the art of associating together. We live in a time of change, and it has a truly explosive quality coming from the new faith by which men nowadays live—the faith in man's capacity to do anything on earth that he really wants to do. Here is the strange new religion, with its own miracle workers and sublime portents. Man's ingenuity will solve every problem and surmount every obstacle, and technological prowess is at last the truly inexhaustible resource that can never be used up. Man can literally do whatever he wants to do.

Here is what can finally set discontents aflame: a race that can put living men on the moon, unlock the fearful power that binds the atoms together, and devise factories where machines do all the work, tot up all the figures, and obediently carry out all proper programs, can assuredly give all people more than enough of every imaginable necessity. This may be a mistaken

3. Tocqueville, *Democracy in America,* II:116, 118.

belief, but it comes, inevitably, out of the new gospel of man's infinite capacity. A society that is based on a firm conviction that there is a blessed abundance of good things and that the supply will never fail is under the most profound pressure to justify its faith by good works. If it fails to do this, it will explode.

For the modern world is one in which all stakes are raised to infinity; win it all or lose it all, in this or the next generation. Man's problem is that he has at last become master of his own fate, and he may not have had the proper training; which is to say that he has arranged things so that he has no one but himself to rely upon. Instead of looking beyond the skies, he is obliged to look into his own heart. If he looks earnestly enough, he may find there the thing he needs most of all—the secret of the art of associating together.

Suggestions for Further Reading

This reading list is offered for the benefit of readers who may wish further information on various matters covered in the text. It does not pretend to be exhaustive; it simply lists a number of books the writer found helpful, in the thought that they may be equally helpful to others.

Barnes, Al. *Vinegar Pie and Other Tales of the Grand Traverse Region.* Detroit, 1959.

Blackbird, Andrew J. *History of the Ottawa and Chippewa Indians of Michigan.* Ypsilanti, Mich., 1887. Reprint: The Little Traverse Regional Historical Society, n.d.

Caruso, John Anthony. *The Great Lakes Frontier.* Indianapolis: The Bobbs-Merrill Co., 1961.

Dunbar, Willis Frederick. *All Aboard! A History of Railroads in Michigan.* Grand Rapids, Mich.: The William B. Eerdmans Publishing Co., 1969.

Dunbar, Willis F. *Kalamazoo and How It Grew.* Kalamazoo: The School of Graduate Studies, Western Michigan University, 1969.

Fitting, James E. *The Archaeology of Michigan.* Garden City, N.Y.: The Natural History Press, 1970.

Fitzmaurice, John W. *The Shanty Boy, or Life in a Lumber Camp.* Cheboygan, Mich.: Democrat Steam Print, 1889. Facsimile reprint: Mt. Pleasant, Mich.: Central Michigan University Press, n.d.

Fuller, George R., editor. *Historic Michigan.* 3 vols. Lansing, Mich.: The National Historical Association, 1924.

Hulbert, William D. *White Pine Days on the Taquamenon.* Lansing, Mich.: The Historical Society of Michigan, 1949.

Lutes, Della. *The Country Kitchen.* Boston: Little, Brown and Co., 1939.

Lutz, William W. *The News of Detroit.* Boston: Little, Brown and Co., 1973.

Havighurst, Walter. *The Long Ships Passing*. New York: The Macmillan Co., 1942.

McKee, Russell. *Great Lakes Country*. New York: Thomas Y. Crowell Co., 1966.

May, George, and Herbert Brinks, editors. *A Michigan Reader: 11,000 B.C. to A.D. 1865*. Grand Rapids: Eerdmans Publishing Co., 1974.

Martin, John Bartlow. *Call It North Country*. New York: Alfred A. Knopf, 1949.

Peterson, William R. *The View from Courthouse Hill*. Philadelphia: Dorrance and Co., 1972.

Nevins, Allan. *Ford: The Times, the Man, the Company*. 3 vols. New York: Charles Scribner's Sons, 1954.

Parkman, Francis. *The Conspiracy of Pontiac*. Boston: Little, Brown and Co., 1901.

Peckham, Howard. *Pontiac and the Indian Uprising*. New York: Russell & Russell, 1970.

Quaife, Milo. *Lake Michigan*. Indianapolis: The Bobbs-Merrill Co., 1948.

Quinby, George Irving. *Indian Life in the Upper Great Lakes*. Chicago: The University of Chicago Press, 1960.

Reimann, Lewis C. *When Pine Was King*. Ann Arbor: Northwoods Publishers, 1952.

Schoolcraft, Henry R. *Narrative Journal of Travels*. East Lansing, Mich., 1953.

Tocqueville, Alexis de. *Democracy in America,* translated by Henry Reeve. 2 vols. New York: G. Dearborn & Co., Etc., 1838.

Warner, Robert, and C. Warren Vanderhill, editors. *A Michigan Reader, 1865 to the Present*. Grand Rapids: William B. Eerdmans Publishing Co., 1974.

Index